PRAISE FOR FIGHTING CHANCE

"Absorbing and brilliant! Over 22 years ago I shared the ring with Alicia Doyle...twice. *Fighting Chance* transported me back to relive those experiences from HER perspective. It was amazing! I highly recommend this book!"

— "Amazing" LAYLA MCCARTER, 8 time, 5 division Boxing World Champion & California Boxing Hall of Fame Inductee

"No punches pulled by the hard-hitting Ms. Doyle in her true life novelistic rendering of what it's like to punch her way to fame! A knockout!!"

— IVOR DAVIS, Investigative Journalist & Best-Selling Author of *Manson Exposed: A Reporter's 50-Year Journey into Madness and Murder*

"Alicia Doyle is a shining example of an individual who continues to fight to save herself from the dark side of life by mentoring troubled young children at Kid Gloves. She is their guiding light, a light that doesn't often shine for them. *Fighting Chance* is exactly that, a chance to survive in the ring and in life. A must read..."

— ROD HOLCOMB, Producer/Director

"Alicia instilled what Kid Gloves Boxing teaches—the A.B.C. Backwards: Conceive, Believe, Achieve. Building CONFIDENCE in all she does, round by round. A true role model for all."

— ROBERT ORTIZ SR., owner of Kid Gloves Boxing

FIGHTING CHANCE

based on a true story

a nonfiction novel by Two-Time Golden Gloves Champion

ALICIA DOYLE

FIGHTING CHANCE
Published by Alicia Doyle Journalist, Inc., Ventura California, USA

First edition

This novel is based on a true story. Some names have been changed to protect the privacy of the individuals included in this story.

Author services by Pedernales Publishing, LLC.
www.pedernalespublishing.com

Author photos on front and back cover: Kathy Cruts

Library of Congress Control Number: 2020900587

ISBN 978-1-7345085-2-9 Paperback Edition
ISBN 978-1-7345085-1-2 Hardcover Edition
ISBN 978-1-7345085-0-5 Digital Edition

Printed in the United States of America

For those who stay in the fight…

FIGHTING CHANCE

CONTENTS

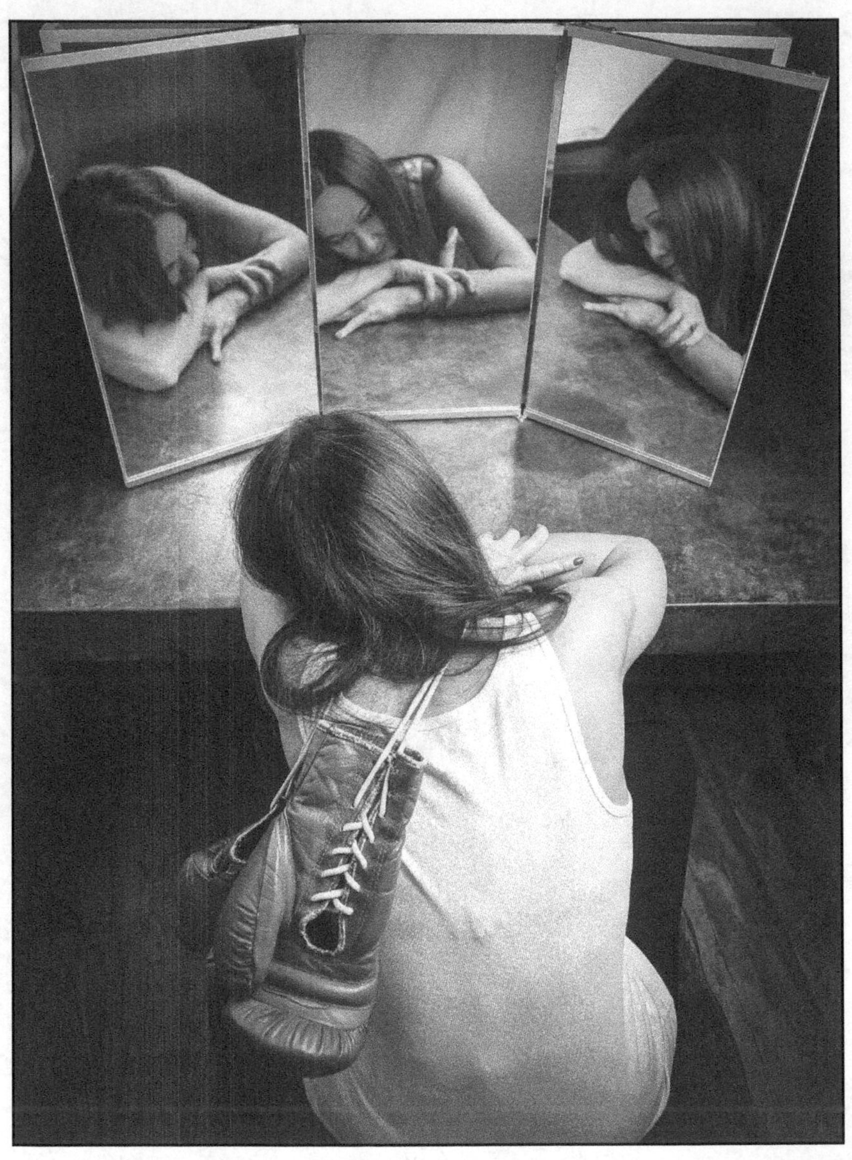

Portrait taken by Kathy Cruts in 2020.

PROLOGUE: DISASTER DIVA

"It's easy to do anything in victory. It's in defeat that a man reveals himself."—Floyd Patterson

Before I started boxing at age twenty-eight, I viewed the sport as the dark side. My paradigm shifted in 1998 when I worked as a newspaper journalist and went on assignment at a boxing gym that served at-risk youth. While reporting this story, I fell in love with boxing, and for the next two years, fought competitively as one of only a few hundred women in America in this male-dominated sport. I earned my ring name—"Disaster Diva"—early on in the game for winning two Golden Gloves Championship titles and three wins by knockout. When I turned pro in 2000, I joined a small group of professional women boxers in the United States, and my pro debut at age thirty earned a place in history as the California Female Fight of the Year.

In the boxing gym, surrounded by men, I broke out of my comfort zone to earn respect for my athletic ability. This task required stripping away my femininity and the insecurities associated with being a woman in their world. I shed blood, sweat and tears alongside them, and worked twice as hard to prove myself before they accepted me as one of their own. The point is—and this is necessary to understand the difference between male and female fighters—in the boxing ring, men take for granted they are men. Women never forget they are women in this masculine space where femininity and fighting is a paradox.

Boxing is described as a noble art of self-defense, the sweet science, a channel for courage, determination and self-discipline. Boxing combines athleticism with skill, strength and artistry, and those who stay with boxing learn important skills for life: focus, heart and dedication—and how to get up when knocked down. I never expected boxing to infuse my psyche emotionally, spiritually and mentally, and put me on a path toward enlightenment. To this day, the skills I discovered in the ring translate to everyday life. I learned that the fight starts from within—and when faced head-on with conviction, honesty, vulnerability and faith, the battle is sublime.

1 STANDING EIGHT

"A champion is someone who gets up when he can't."
—Jack Dempsey

On the day of my first exhibition match, the newly built Boys & Girls Club in Simi Valley smelled of fresh paint, the carpet barely walked upon. A small crowd filled the main gym where alongside the boxing ring, one-foot-tall plastic trophies, each topped with the shape of a boy boxer in a fighting stance painted in fake gold, lined up in four rows upon a collapsible table.

Robert Ortiz, owner of a boxing gym for at-risk youth called Kid Gloves, rented the space for the show, where boxers from gyms all over the San Fernando Valley came to compete, but no other girls had shown up to fight. I trained for weeks to prepare, but felt a sense of relief when no match was made for me. The closer the clock ticked to boxing time, the bigger the crowd grew, and the fights were about to start when *she* walked in. From the back, Layla looked like a guy, shorter than me, a dirty-blond with short hair and broad, muscular shoulders. She looked strong, but not cut like me. My body was lean, muscles popping, from training six days a week and dropping weight for the fight.

This will be easy, I assumed, believing Layla wasn't training as hard as I was.

Whispers through the crowd told otherwise. This nineteen-year-old was a kickboxing champ, a veteran in the ring facing off with me, a newbie with zero experience. Hell, I didn't even know what an exhibition was until my cornerman and trainer, Stan Ward—known as "Coach" in the boxing circuit—explained it.

"You'll wear protective headgear and fourteen-ounce gloves, and go three two-minute rounds. The exhibition will be good practice to prepare you for a real match. The fight isn't scored. It doesn't go on the books."

"So it's a fight…but not really a fight?"

Coach nodded yes. "You need the experience. This will be great for you. We also need to find out where you're at."

"You mean physically? I'm in better shape than I've ever been in my life."

"No. I need to see if you have the mental strength for battle with someone who wants to take you out."

I was all in until the day of my exhibition, when I felt a level of fear I've never felt before. I had trained for months with men in the boxing gym, where they punched me over and over again during practice, but this was different. Here, I could get hurt or knocked out. I knew I couldn't afford mental defeat before stepping in the ring, so I reassured myself there's no way Layla was training as hard as I was, and there's no way this *teenager* can hit harder than the guys. Then I learned more. My opponent was from Washington State, and was staying in Simi Valley with Victor and Shannon, Robert's brother and sister-in-law.

Fuck. I'm being set up to get my clock cleaned, I thought to myself.

I had met Victor and Shannon while writing about Kid Gloves as a journalist at the *Ventura County Star*. While reporting the story, which made me fall in love with boxing, I became acquainted with Victor, a pro boxer, and Shannon, an aspiring amateur fighter. Soon after I entered their world, the competition grew fierce between Shannon and me. We were around the same age, in the same weight class, and both trained at Kid Gloves. We both wanted the same thing: to be boxing champs. But instead of supporting each other as women in a male-dominated sport, our rivalry caused dissension. Shannon was family, I was an outsider, and the jealousy sparked when I came out of nowhere as an up-and-coming boxer at Kid Gloves. Though Shannon had skills, I surpassed her in physical challenges at the boxing gym, like skipping rope for half an hour straight, hitting the speed bag for ten rounds, running five miles a day, and smacking the focus mitts to the point of exhaustion. At Kid Gloves, face to face, Shannon and I were cordial, but the pleasantries didn't wash the dirty looks and gossip we dished behind each other's backs. When I saw Victor and Shannon escort Layla through the Boys & Girls Club, Shannon pointed at me, and whispered something in Layla's ear. Coach saw the fear on my face, put his hands on my shoulders, and turned my gaze.

"Alicia. Focus."

I couldn't. The fear sent visceral surges from my heart through my veins and caused so much discomfort, I wanted to jump out of my skin.

The slightest bit of relief came over me when I heard Layla had partied the night before.

Good…maybe she has a hangover, I thought.

I didn't want Layla to see how much she scared me, and put on a poker face the best I could. She remained calm, made her way through the crowd, shook hands, and gave hugs to fans who showed up to see her box. Layla had a huge following, and I sensed an intense hatred from people who, for whatever reason, didn't like me. Whether they were from rival gyms or clans, or Layla's supporters who wanted to see me go down, I can't say. But the feeling was tangible.

After a few of the men's bouts, the referee motioned for Layla and me to step into the ring. We wore our tight-fitting safety headgear and fourteen-ounce boxing gloves. I tried to look brave, but felt awkward in my knee-length boxing shorts, and constricted in the plastic protective breast cups strapped to my chest. We stepped inside the ring, then went to our corners. Rich Riley, a retired pro boxer and one of my mentors and sparring partners, stood in the center of the ring, raised both arms toward each of us in opposite corners, and motioned us forward with a slight gesture of his fingers. I saw the crowd—bigger than before at ringside—from the corner of my eye. In that moment, I wanted out.

"The girls are fighting!"

"This'll be good!"

"Kick her ass, Layla!"

I pretended not to hear the catcalls when my opponent and I stood face-to-face and Rich told us the rules. Layla and I fixated on each other's eyes when I nodded in acknowledgment to Rich, even though I hadn't heard a word. He sent us back to our corners to wait for the starting bell, and when it tolled, we'd go toe-to-toe. While in my corner for those few moments, Coach gave me instructions, but I didn't hear those either, as my heart beat out of my chest. I had trouble catching my breath and started to hyperventilate when the starting bell rang and echoed through the rafters. We moved toward each other at the center of the ring, where Layla seemed so calm, like she was right at home.

One thought went through my mind: *Fuck, get me out of here!*

For the first few seconds, we swapped punches evenly, or so it seemed. But Layla got the upper hand from the start, and hit me harder than I've ever been hit before. It's impossible to convey what getting punched in the face feels like to someone who's never felt this pain. You don't know unless you've been there. Simple comparisons, like hitting your thumb with a hammer, *might* be similar on the pain-factor scale, but give no justice to getting hit with a closed fist in the face. I never felt the level of pain Layla inflicted, the hurt she imposed over and over again, or the rush of adrenaline that ran so high, I didn't have time to process the hurt before being socked in the liver with her straight right, punched in the nose with her jab, or smacked in the cheek with her left hook.

Less than a minute into the first round, I feared she had caused permanent damage. I couldn't believe her effortless strength that made me want to leave that ring, to go straight home, and never box again. Finally, my instincts kicked in, and forced me to raise my gloves in front of my face to survive. But Layla broke through my barrier with ease, and overpowered me with speed, strength, and accuracy.

I look like an idiot, I thought, as I flailed like a scared kid on the playground fighting the school bully.

Layla fought like a pro, strategically picked her punches and slipped most of mine, which were meager at best, more like a swarm of annoying flies than boxing combinations. Then she cracked me straight on the nose.

Fuck! My face!

In these moments, I possessed zero control, zero ability to execute all I had learned in so many months of training. I felt like a fool, a moron with a pipe dream, an idiot with an unattainable goal of disillusionment that I could survive.

About halfway into the first round, I lost all strength to keep my gloves up, making it easier for Layla to punch, connect and score in this so-called exhibition that didn't go on the books.

The crowd went wild, screamed in favor of Layla, and laughed at me for getting my ass kicked so early in the fight. Rich saw I was in danger of getting knocked out, stopped the fight and sent Layla to her corner. The crowd stood and roared, celebrating my opponent's obvious victory.

Amateur exhibition, my ass, I thought. *This fight is real.*

Dizzy and out of breath, I wanted to quit, but my pride wouldn't let me. Boxers who had trained me were watching—how could I quit in front of these guys? I worked so hard to earn their respect, to make my mark as a woman in their world. And I refused to give my enemies the satisfaction of seeing me fall.

Rich stood before me, face-to-face, in the middle of the ring. He held up eight fingers to give me a standing eight count, a boxing judgment call made by a referee during a bout. When invoked, the ref stops the action and counts down from eight, and during that time will decide if the failing boxer can go on. After the count, Rich would decide if I could keep fighting without serious injury.

Counting backwards, he held up eight fingers before me, folding them back one at a time.

"Eight!"

I heard the crowd cheer.

"Seven!"

Fighting back tears, I felt blood pulsate to Layla's blows.

"Six!"

I saw Layla in her corner watching me.

"Five!"

I struggled to catch my breath.

"Four!"

The pain from Layla's punches grew worse. I wanted to quit.

"Three!"

I wasn't knocked out yet, might as well go all the way.

"Two!"

"One!"

I was still standing, still alive. Layla didn't take me out, and to my surprise, I was ready to go again. Rich cupped the cheeks on my headgear, and looked me in the eyes.

"Are you okay?" he asked with fatherly concern—the same concern he had shown when he hit me too hard while we were sparring in the months we trained together.

I nodded yes.

"Are you sure?"

"Yes, I'm sure."

But I was scared shitless, and the last thing I wanted was to feel Layla punch me again. At the same time, the thought of quitting scared me more. I refused to allow my haters watch me crumble in defeat, even though I was in a world of hurt.

Rich walked to Layla's corner.

"Ease up," he told her. She nodded, took a drink of water, and didn't need a wipe down because she barely broke a sweat.

When I walked back to my corner to wait for the next round, Coach was not happy.

"What are you doing?!" he barked as he grabbed me by the shoulders with his massive hands and shook me.

His tough love worked with the guys—it gave them the juice to kick ass. But I wanted Coach to say everything was going to be okay, it wasn't as bad as I thought, and I was doing pretty well, even though I was getting my butt kicked.

He told me how to proceed: Throw a left hook when Layla dropped her right hand, slip when she threw a jab, block with my gloves when she used my face as a target.

"I'll try, Coach," I responded with tears in my eyes, unable to pay full attention, knowing I had to go through it all again in a matter of seconds.

When the bell rang for round two, Layla backed off, but only a bit. She pulled her punches in terms of strength, so my head didn't snap back with whiplash each time she took a shot. But she outpunched me again like a champ before we walked back to our corners for another thirty-second rest.

"That was better," Coach told me. "But you're still gettin' hit too much."

"No shit!"

"Just breathe. Deep. In and out."

"I don't think I can go again."

"You can. Just one more round. You can do this."

The last and final round was just as scary as the first two, and it seemed like Layla got better each time. For me, every round felt like eternity—a mere 120 seconds per round felt like forever in slow motion. Layla prevailed in the end, but failed to cost me another standing eight. I got in a few mediocre shots, and whether Layla allowed that or not, I don't know. But she would have won if this fight was real, and knocked me out in round one if the ref didn't step in. I was outfought, outclassed.

When the fight was over, we got a standing ovation and plastic trophies for participating. We left the ring and went our separate ways, without saying a word to each other. I headed straight for the women's bathroom to see the damage in the mirror. On the way, to my surprise, the guys congratulated me. I thought I'd get heat for the standing eight. But one gave me a dozen red roses, and others gave me high-fives and hugs.

"Not many people have what it takes to step in that square," one boxer told me.

"You did great!" said another.

Still, I wanted the win. Even though the match didn't count on the books, I wanted to take Layla out. I wanted to prove something to myself, to the crowd, to the haters who wanted to see me hurt. Why, I can't say.

"You are already a winner," another boxer consoled. "You got in there. That makes you a winner."

Coach approached me with open arms and praise. He was a drill sergeant while working in my corner. But after the fight, his gentle way returned.

"The real test was just getting in there."

"Then why do I feel so shitty about it?"

"There's nothing to feel bad about. Don't be hard on yourself."

"Is it always this hard?"

"Boxing *is* hard. That's why not many people do it, men or women. What you did is remarkable."

"I don't feel remarkable. I got my ass kicked."

"Yes. You fought a tough girl. But you stayed in there. Didn't quit. When things got hard, you didn't walk away."

His words didn't ease the pain of losing. I lowered my head in shame as I entered the restroom and looked in the mirror, where my reflection shocked me. All that pain I felt in the ring—all those punches that left me in tears—made few marks, with only a few spots around my eyes starting to swell with purple and blue bruises underneath. My nose, which I thought Layla broke, was intact. There was no blood.

I removed my sweat-drenched boxing shorts and top, washed my face, and removed the tight rubber bands from my braids, loosening my long hair. I slipped on my white jeans and black leather vest, laced up my Doc Martens, and dabbed red gloss on my lips. I walked out of that restroom like nothing happened. I was exhausted, in tremendous pain, yet exhilarated. That fight was one of the greatest thrills of my life. The adrenaline high of surviving was a feeling I had never felt before.

Coach told me to rest for a few days, then get back to the

boxing gym for more training. He revealed that he had signed me up for my first official amateur match—the National Blue & Gold championship, sanctioned by USA Boxing—a few months away. The thought of fighting again terrified me. But the adrenaline high of enduring a fight was an instant addiction. That night, I nursed my aching body with a hot shower, six Ibuprofen and seven hours of sleep. When I looked back on the match, the standing eight stood out the most, those eight seconds that felt like an eternity, those few moments that barely marked time. I thought I was defeated. I thought I couldn't go on. But I found the strength.

Portrait taken by Kathy Cruts in 2020.

2

KID GLOVES

"The hero and the coward both feel the same thing, but the hero uses his fear, projects it onto his opponent, while the coward runs. It's the same thing, fear, but it's what you do with it that matters."—Cus D'Amato

About a year before I stepped into the ring, the spark that lit my fire for boxing happened when I was working alone in the newsroom late one night at the *Ventura County Star*, where I covered crime, education and nonprofit organizations in Simi Valley. The phone at the receptionist's desk rang, and with everyone gone for the day, I answered. The caller, a community activist in town, told me about Kid Gloves, a boxing gym in a strip mall flooded by a storm caused by El Niño, which was regarded as one of the most powerful rain events in recorded history, resulting in natural disasters across the globe. She emphasized that Kid Gloves was the only place of its kind in Simi Valley, a lily-white suburban town—and more important the gym served at-risk youth. These special gym members were mostly Latinos and latchkey kids who'd be out wreaking havoc if it weren't for Kid Gloves, where they could train for free alongside boxing champs, as long as they finished their homework, remained clean and sober, avoided cursing, and respected those around them.

I never liked boxing for its brutality, and was turned off as soon as I heard the pitch. I told the woman I wasn't interested and would pass the story along to our sports writer, but she persisted. She followed my articles, especially my writings about nonprofits in town that worked for the greater good.

"You're the one to write this story."

"I don't know anything about boxing. Our sports writer is a better fit."

After a long pause, she pushed.

"Think of the youths. Without Kid Gloves, they have nowhere else to go. These aren't the kind of kids who go to the Boys & Girls Club. These kids are different. These kids are troubled. They need more than arts and crafts to keep them occupied, keep them off the streets."

My view of boxing at the time was largely influenced by my mother, who once told me fighting was "the dark side." As for boxing specifically, she believed hurting another for fame or money was a sin. But the woman on the phone continued to coax me.

"Good press will help raise money so Kid Gloves can re-open in another spot in town. If not, these kids have nowhere to go. They'll be up to no good."

Rolling my eyes, reluctantly I agreed.

"Okay. Who's the contact to set up an interview?"

She gave me the name and number of the owner, Robert Ortiz, and skepticism raced through my brain. I wondered if he'd have a flat nose and cauliflower ears, if he'd be a womanizer, a pig, a complete jerk. These feelings compounded when Robert arrived for our interview nearly an hour late. My photographer and I were about to leave when a two-door Honda Civic pulled up and a clean-shaven Mexican-American in his late thirties, doused in heavy cologne, stepped out.

"I'm so sorry to keep you waiting," Robert said as he rushed to unlock the door and lead us into the gym.

When we walked in, the lights were broken, but the sunlight filtered through dirty windows, illuminating the rubble. Everything Robert had built and paid for with multiple loans and a second mortgage on his home the storm had destroyed when rainwater broke through the roof. I noticed the boxing ring where the matches took place, a fifteen-by-fifteen-foot square set on a raised platform. At each corner of the ring stood a post, all surrounded by four parallel rows of ropes, which Robert meticulously wrapped by hand in red, white and blue tape. I wondered what this ring looked like before the flood hit, ruining his creation, now tattered and hanging by threads. The memorabilia on the walls was also soaked: photographs autographed by Muhammad Ali and Oscar de la Hoya, boxing gloves signed by Smokin' Joe Frazier, and other keepsakes Robert collected over his lifetime. But he didn't care about this stuff.

"The worst thing is, the kids have nowhere to go," he said as his eyes brimmed with tears. "Sometimes I feel like giving up. But I can't give up because of the kids."

"What do you mean?"

"I always teach them to never, never quit. Now, I have to practice what I preach."

I was surprised at the depth of compassion of this man, whom I wrongly pegged before meeting him in person. He genuinely cared about these at-risk kids, getting them off the streets, giving them a positive space and outlet for whatever they were going through.

My article about Robert's plight ran on the front page of the newspaper, pulling the heartstrings of the Simi Valley community, and, several months later, Kid Gloves reopened in a different location on the other side of town. Keeping up the momentum, I covered the grand opening of the new gym, and my heart opened to the boxing world even wider. I interviewed a teen under house arrest, another who battled to stay clean and sober; one boy's father was incarcerated, and others survived emotional and physical abuse at the hands of their supposed protectors. One thing they shared in common was Kid Gloves, the one place they felt safe and welcome despite their circumstances, and, despite their broken pieces, received acceptance and unconditional love.

"At Kid Gloves everyone's a champion," Robert often told the kids. "You never really know what's going to happen in life. But if you stay focused on your goal, it will happen if you believe in yourself."

Though I was a journalist covering the story, nobody knew how much I empathized with these kids. Their stories felt parallel to my past, filled with pain and uncertainty. They didn't know I witnessed my first act of violence at age five, felt the heartbreak of my parents' divorce, and survived a suicide attempt at age thirteen. But more about my origin story later. The point is—pain is pain, regardless of the situation. And while boxing equates with pain, the pain in the ring is superficial.

"Boxing isn't about hurting others or getting hurt," Robert once told me. "Boxers face their own fears. It's about learning to let go of your own insecurities."

After I saw the impact of the first story I wrote about Kid Gloves, I delved deeper, and wrote a two-part series that explored the inner workings of the gym with a focus on its people. I compiled interviews with fighters, volunteer coaches, parents, Robert's family and the kids. I learned that boxing has been called "a gentleman's sport" for superior athletes. I learned that boxing is a sport that instills courage, determination and confidence—and, surprise to me, humility. While my fondness for the sport grew while writing these stories, I never considered getting involved, even though Robert repeatedly urged me to take his aerobic boxing class.

"There's zero contact. Don't worry, you won't get hit," he said, emphasizing, "it's also a great workout."

"Thanks, but I already take Tae Bo," I replied, referring to a fitness routine popular at the time, incorporating martial arts moves into aerobics-style exercise. It was developed by Taekwondo expert Billy Blanks, whose studio was down the street from my bungalow apartment in Sherman Oaks in the San Fernando Valley, about forty-five minutes away from Kid Gloves.

"Trust me. My boxing class is a lot harder than Tae Bo. When you're ready, we're here for you."

Soon after my two-part series about Kid Gloves was published, I went through a volatile breakup with a boyfriend I suspected was cheating. I confirmed this fact with our mutual friend, drove to his house to break up in person, and saw the other woman's car in his driveway. The two of them were out on his doorstep, engaged in intimate conversation, and I drove by slowly to make sure he saw me catch him in the act. The anger that boiled through my veins felt like a volcano of rage waiting to erupt. As soon as he saw me, he left the girl's side, jumped in his car, and followed me down the street. He honked nonstop, waved his left arm out his window, and motioned me to stop on an overpass bridge. I pulled over, curious what he had to say, but more intent on telling him off. He got out of his car and approached mine on the driver's side.

"*Please* give me another chance. It's not what you think."

"I'm not stupid." I avoided eye contact and looked straight ahead.

"Listen to me!" He yelled so loud I recoiled when the words pierced my left ear.

"No! We're done!"

I didn't expect what he did next. With his right closed fist, he punched my left cheek. I grasped my face with both hands, and he forced his slender body into my car through my open window, and slid into my passenger's seat.

"*Please*, just listen to me!"

"Get out of my car!" I demanded, with a level of rage I never felt in my life. He punched me again, this time with his left fist.

"Stop hitting me, you asshole! Get the fuck out of my car!"

He realized what he had done, got out of my car, and I sped away crying. The weird thing is, after all that, I still cared about him and wished we could have worked things out. Part of me also wondered if I did something wrong, that I deserved the beating. Then my sadness turned to rage, not toward him, but myself. I was furious that I allowed myself to become a statistic, a weak woman in an abusive relationship. I was so angry, I felt like hitting something hard—over and over again. The feeling was unshakable.

The next day, I showed up at Kid Gloves, my eyes red from crying the night before, my face swollen from being punched on both sides. Robert welcomed me to my first cardio boxing class, where I'd get to pummel a heavy bag as hard as I could for an hour, exhaust myself, and clear my head. Robert had gotten to know me a bit over the many months I came into his gym as a reporter. He knew something was wrong the moment I walked in.

"Are you okay?"

"I'm here to take your class," I replied, coldly, not looking him in the eye.

He took me by the hand and led me to the side of the ring, where he sat me down and told me to wait as he went to grab a pair of new fourteen-ounce blue boxing gloves.

"My gift to you…for all you've done for us," he said, handing them over to me with such kindness, my eyes swelled up with tears.

He must have known I'd gone through *something* I didn't want to talk about, because he didn't ask any more questions. Instead, he wrapped my hands in gauze to protect them.

"This will keep your hands from breaking," he explained, and slipped my wrapped fists into the gloves.

As I watched him meticulously wrap my hands, I remembered what I had learned about him during all those months of reporting. Robert, whose ring name in his heyday was "Too Sweet," knew his way around the fight practice. A stocky, powerful guy, he and his brother Danny Ortiz were crowd favorites at the Country Club, a concert and boxing venue in the San Fernando Valley during the 1980s. Robert went 7-4-1 as a bantamweight before retiring. Danny, known in the ring as "Big Shorty," finished with a 22-4 record in his career as a lightweight. These thoughts raced through my mind as I looked at more than a dozen punching bags hanging from the ceiling with just enough peripheral space for one person each. I took a blue bag in the front row, so I could watch Robert's cues up close. He turned on the music, techno with a heavy bass beat, quickening my adrenaline, filling me with excitement to hit the bag. After the warm-up came the punching drills. Left, right. Left, right, left. Left hook, right. Over and over again. Robert saw my intensity right away.

"You don't have to hit the bag so hard. Be careful, or you'll hurt yourself."

"I'm good," I replied, huffing and puffing.

I felt anything but hurt. The physical exertion of punching that bag as hard as I could gave me a rush, a sense of elation. All the heartache I felt the day prior from the breakup, all the rage that pulsed through my veins, transcended into a natural high.

For the next two weeks, Monday through Saturday, I took Robert's class. By week three, I was taking two classes back to back, sometimes three in a row.

"You're crazy," a gym member told me in front of Robert. "How do you have so much energy?"

"She's a beast," he replied for me. "She's the Energizer Bunny of the gym."

I knew the fuel for my workouts was anger, and Robert's classes became my escape. The harder and longer I hit the bag, the more exhausted I became, leaving little energy to contemplate my pain and regrets. The less time I had to think, the better I slept at night, and before I knew it, all I could think about was getting back inside the boxing gym. In a few months, my body adjusted to three aerobic boxing classes in a row, six days a week. I wanted more. So I started watching the boxers and studying their moves. Quietly from the sidelines, I watched them spar, skip rope, hit the speed bag, and shadowbox. Then, on my own, I mimicked them, and trained solo as the music from Robert's cardio boxing class played in the background.

At first, training my body in the physical unknown felt completely awkward. Bobbing and weaving, shuffling front and back while keeping my hands up to protect my face, standing in a boxing stance, are unfamiliar moves to the human body. But I became a quick learner, and because I trained hard like the guys, I stood out and people started to notice—especially trainers looking for a girl boxer. Back then, few women boxed, so having a girl fighter was considered a major asset. It wasn't long before a few coaches saw my intensity in the gym, and approached me about boxing competitively. I was blind to this attention initially, because all I wanted to do was train and quiet the screaming demons in my mind. But the better I became, the more my desire grew to box competitively, and the more my presence became known in the gym, the more coaches started to approach me. I couldn't help but wonder what it would be like to box, so I started giving the idea more serious thought. With all these coaches telling me how good I'd be at the sport, why not give it a shot? Boxing would give me a chance to show off my strength. Knocking out an opponent would prove I'm a woman *not* to be fucked with.

I decided to do it, and came up with an action plan. I knew I needed the *best* coach, someone who'd take me seriously and care about my safety in the ring, because boxing is dangerous, leaving cuts and bruises at best, and permanent brain damage or death at worst. I also knew mediocrity wasn't an option: if I was going to be a contender, I wanted to be among the best, meaning I needed to learn from the best trainers to earn my place as a woman fighter. Robert introduced me to boxing through Kid Gloves, so I approached him first. He trained and managed several male fighters, including his son, so I thought he'd be perfect. I assumed he'd jump at the chance to train me, to prepare me for competition, making him one of the few male trainers with a girl fighter. But his reply felt like a sucker punch.

"You're too pretty to box."

Portrait taken by J.E. Neuhaus at Kid Gloves Boxing Gym in Simi Valley, California, in 1999.

3

COACH'S GIRL

"When a person's interested in something, they're willing to tolerate any kind of problems that may come up."—Cus D'Amato

Crazy enough, it was just about that time that women's boxing was moving in from out of the far fringe of the sports world. The earliest documented account of what would later be called a "female event" was in 1722, when a fighter named Elizabeth Wilkinson called herself the "European Championess" and staged a match in London. Elizabeth was a bare-knuckle brawler who fought both men and women, and challenged Hannah Hyfield to a match that would require them to clutch a coin in each hand to prevent scratching and eye-gouging. Four years later, she fought Mary Welsh of Ireland in a match advertised to stress the professionalism of the encounter: The boxers would wear full civilian attire, "including petticoats," as opposed to most other female fighters of the day—prostitutes who commonly boxed topless.

Elizabeth was from a working class background, and shared a last name with prizefighter Robert Wilkinson, a thief and murderer executed the same year that Elizabeth fought Hannah. However, historians speculate that she may not have been married to him, but simply took the name to exploit Robert's notoriety. She was later referred to as Elizabeth Stokes, and fought alongside her husband James. They challenged other couples—James boxed the man and Elizabeth took on the woman.

About 150 years later, in 1876, history records that the first official female boxing match in the United States was at New York Hills Theater. Nell Saunders and Rose Harland fought it out for the top prize: a silver butter dish. A generation after that, men's and women's boxing were presented at the 1904 Olympics in St. Louis as display events. Boxing then became an Olympic sport, but only for men. Another milestone: the first-ever televised female match featured Barbara Buttrick in 1954; she fought as a ninety-eight-pound flyweight at four feet, eleven inches tall.

In the decades that followed, pioneering women fought for their right to fight. Carnival-type spectacles of topless bouts continued in Europe and North America, on tour and in bars, but the sport was also branching out, and the athletes fought to be taken seriously. Harlem lightweight Marian Trimiar, an African-American who shaved her head and adopted the ring name "Lady Tyger," staged a month-long hunger strike in 1987 to demand better pay and working conditions for lady pugilists. The Smithsonian later requested her memorabilia; but it was only in 1993 that USA Boxing lifted a ban on women's boxing, and the next year, the Amateur International Boxing Association did the same. The stars were falling into alignment. Christy Martin fought Deirdre Gogarty in 1996, a match that's considered the birth of the golden age of women's boxing. Soon after, stars such as Christy, Lucia Rijker, Mia St. John and Muhammad Ali's daughter Laila turned into marquee names.

And that's where I came in.

TOO PRETTY TO BOX: what does that mean? I didn't understand Robert's reaction. What does my reflection in the mirror have to do with me wanting to box like the women trailblazers who came before me, making my own mark in history? So I kept on training, as hard as I could. I welcomed the exhaustion and my outward transformation. With each passing day, my body grew stronger and leaner, a physicality which transcended to a growing inner strength that I never expected. On an athletic level, boxing is all about conditioning the body for power, endurance and stamina, and behind all this, the mind must also be strong, because if the mind is defeated, the body will follow. These reflections reminded me of the metaphysical church my mother joined when I was twelve, where I learned about the power of the mind. I never thought these teachings had an effect on me, but here they were again. Whether in church, in life, or in the boxing ring, the same rule applies: "The more power one gives to his thought, the more power will it have."

This rule doesn't discriminate or involve judgment of any kind, making it rather simple: positive thoughts lead to positive outcomes, and negative thoughts lead to negative outcomes—in other words, cause and effect. While training, which would ultimately translate how I executed my skills in the ring, I couldn't afford to have negative thoughts going through my mind. I had to focus solely on overpowering my opponent, outwitting them with my prowess, outpunching them with combinations, outsmarting them with my strategy.

Each time I trained, my mind and body grew stronger, while providing respite from all I already went through, silencing my emotional trauma from childhood, halting thoughts of weakness from being in an abusive relationship. Memories of my dad's departure, my mom's pernicious neglect, all went by the wayside as I zeroed in on the tasks before me: speed-climbing stairs at a stadium, running up a dirt trail carrying a twenty-pound backpack, pushing out hundreds of sit-ups, sparring grueling rounds with the guys. When Robert told me I was too pretty to box, my desire to fight became more profound than ever, partly because of the anomaly of female fighters, combined with my yearning to see just how far I could go in the sport.

With these thoughts racing through my mind, I was training like a maniac when Stan Ward walked into Kid Gloves. The former heavyweight champion noticed me right away. An imposing black man almost seven feet tall, he said to call him Coach, which was stitched in bright yellow capital letters on the front of his black baseball cap. He introduced himself, and held out his giant right hand, covered in callused knuckles, to shake mine. I took off my boxing glove to expose my sweat-filled hand wrap, and extended my right hand to his. He praised my abilities, and took particular notice of how hard I punched the heavy bag, the force of which caused echoes throughout the gym.

"Would you ever consider competing?" he asked in his gentle, raspy voice.

"I'd love to…but nobody will take me seriously because I'm a girl."

Coach's eyes lit up from the inside out.

"Women's boxing is huge right now. There are only a few hundred women in America boxing professionally."

"That's more than ever, right?"

"Yes. But women still can't box in the Olympics. They're not allowed."

"This is the 1990s. You'd think things would have changed by now."

"Not yet. Women boxers don't get the credibility they deserve as athletes. Maybe you can help change that. You're a great athlete."

"Thank you. I've never been this strong in my life."

"I've seen you train here before. You train harder than a lot of guys. I've been searching for a girl fighter, but someone special. I need a tough girl with brains. Someone well-spoken, someone with guts. I think you'd be great."

We agreed to train a few days a week at Benny the Jet's Gym in Van Nuys. (Named for Benny Urquidez, a karate champ famous for once fighting in a Hong Kong death match challenge. He didn't kill the other guy, but later said when the fight ended, his opponent "looked like the Elephant Man.") The move meant time away from Kid Gloves, the place that felt like home, where I received unconditional love and support from Robert and his training camp.

Coach and I started the next Saturday. I showed up in the same scrappy clothes I wore at Kid Gloves, where Robert called me "the Rocky Balboa of the gym," because my oversized T-shirts and sweatpants were full of holes and masked my feminine build. I never wore makeup, tied my hair back in a tight braid, and from a distance, I could have easily been mistaken for a guy, which happened on several occasions. Like the time I was in the parking lot at Kid Gloves putting my gear in my trunk, and a teenage boy looking for Robert approached me from behind.

"Hey man, is Robert still here?"

When I turned around and spoke, the boy seemed shocked.

"He stepped out for a minute but he'll be back."

"I'm sorry. I thought you were a dude."

Benny the Jet's Gym was vastly different from Kid Gloves, and I had no idea what I was in for. After my warm-up of shadowboxing and skipping rope, Coach put me in the ring to spar round-robin with three boy boxers. These guys were all younger than me, but their strong, lean physiques indicated they had been in the game for some time. And because I was a newbie in their territory, I knew they'd try to take me to school. They didn't want a girl in their house, and because I was the only one, everyone at the gym stopped to watch.

When the starting bell rang, the punches started to fly for two minutes straight. At Kid Gloves, sparring was always a challenge, but the guys took it easy on me by pulling their punches, avoiding hard hits in my face, and knowing when I'd had enough. The guys at Benny's were the opposite: they wanted me out of there, and the only way to get me out was to inflict a world of hurt.

"Keep your hands up!" Coach barked as I got punched in the face over and over again. "Wrong! Better…better! No! You're hit! You're hit!"

The rest bell rang and I went back to my corner. One of the guys hit me square on the nose so hard, I thought he broke it. Looking away from everyone's stares on the sidelines, I wanted to start bawling. But there was no way in hell I'd shed a tear in that ring, especially with all the guys watching, whispering and snickering in the background. Sparring was a huge part of training in preparation for competition, and I knew if I couldn't get past the hurt, I'd never get to the next step. I was used to the guys at Kid Gloves taking it easy on me in the ring, inflating my ego every time I trained, making me believe I'd never feel real pain. But at Benny's, the introduction of pain came quick.

Back in my corner, Coach wiped the sweat from my face with a towel and gave me a swig of water.

"You're gettin' hit too much," he warned me. "You're not bobbin' and weavin'. You gotta get outta the way. Your brain will get scrambled if you keep this up."

Then, for a moment, he broke his seriousness.

"I don't want you to get turned down for doing a commercial later on because you can't read the cue-card."

His joke made me laugh as I caught my breath.

"Okay…time to go again," Coach told me as he motioned the

second boy boxer to enter the ring. The punches flew again for another two minutes, but this time I kept my hands up to protect my face, remembering how hard the first boy hit. The second boy didn't take it easy on me either, and struck me with a few solid shots, but not as many as the boy before.

"Better!" Coach yelled at me from the corner. "Now move, move, move! Get out of the way! Use your jab! You got him! You nailed him! Do it again!"

This training at Benny's all went down before I fought my first exhibition match against Layla, and I returned to Benny's less than a week later. But this time around, the boxing gym felt like home. Now I was known as "Coach's girl," returning as a fighter. Though I spent time training with the guys for weeks on end—shedding blood, sweat and tears alongside them—I still needed to earn respect as a woman in their world. After my match against Layla, I finally reached this goal by sharing their experience of one-on-one battle in the square. Now, we shared something in common that most people on the planet will never understand. For the first time in my life, I felt triumphant, powerful and special.

"You did good today," Coach told me after I survived sparring round robin with the boys.

"Thank you…but that was *hard*. Sometimes, I don't know why I'm doing this. Sometimes I want to quit. But something always brings me back."

Coach paused for a moment and contemplated my words before responding.

"One day, you'll no longer need boxing to tell you who you are."

4 ALWAYS FINISH

"Boxing is a sport of self-control. You must understand fear so you can manipulate it. Fear is like fire. You can make it work for you: it can warm you in the winter, cook your food when you're hungry, give you light when you're in the dark and produce energy. Let it go out of control and it can hurt you, even kill you...Fear is a friend of exceptional people."
—Cus D'Amato

After another exhausting three-hour workout—the only girl among Coach's small cadre of fighters—I sat limp in the center of the ring, sweat-drenched in my tattered black sweatpants and oversized gray T-shirt. The gym was ready to close, with all the weary fighters leaving one by one.

"Thanks, Coach," one boy said, straggling with soreness out the front door.

"See you tomorrow, Coach," said another, pulling a wool cap over his clean-shaven head before stepping into the evening cold.

On their way out, they nodded my way with eye contact, confirming without words that I was one of them. Coach climbed into the ring and got down on one knee to rub the pain from my shoulders. I was still sore and stiff from my fight with Layla, with bruises around my eyes transforming from black and blue to a healing yellow hue.

"You're healing fast."

"I've always been a fast healer."

"Looking back, how do you feel about your first fight?"

"It was scary. But I feel pretty good about it. I didn't quit. I wanted to, but I didn't."

"That was the first time we worked together…in between rounds, when I yelled at you, you didn't like that, did you?"

"No."

"I could tell. It won't happen again. But know this—sometimes I may tell you to do things that make you mad at me. But I'd rather have you mad at me than hurt in the ring."

I thought about the women who just started to earn respect and money in the sport as genuine athletes. But women's boxing still sent mixed signals. Brawlers like Christy Martin, one of the most successful and prominent female boxers in the United States and the person who legitimized women's participation in boxing, were outshined by sex symbols like Mia St. John, a Playboy Playmate who made tens of thousands of dollars fighting four two-minute rounds on the undercard of pro matches. Back then, women in boxing were such an anomaly, whenever female fighters were spoken of, their concept was often fetishized, rather than given the legitimacy they deserved. I was more in Christy's line, trying to earn respect as an athlete—not just eye candy like the ring card girls who strut their stuff in between rounds.

"I can't think when you yell at me," I told Coach.

I remembered all the times my mom and dad fought when I was young, screaming at each other behind the closed doors of their bedroom within earshot of mine. During their fights, I crouched in the corner next to my dresser and clutched my tattered teddy bear, overwhelmed with fear and confusion over the two people I loved the most who were tearing each other apart.

"When you yelled at me between rounds with Layla, I got confused. I know you were trying to give me instructions. I know you meant well. But screaming at me didn't work."

Coach nodded his head.

"I'm used to yelling at the guys. They respond. They execute. But you and I, we'll find what works for us."

Coach was a fierce giant in the ring, gentled by years of pushing his mind and body to the limit in battle. As my trainer, he exuded inner peace, a sense of calm I needed in my corner. The exhibition against Layla was my initiation, which Coach facilitated. One of the first lessons I learned from him: always finish—no matter what it takes.

"You survived the standing eight," he reassured me. "I knew you would. You're a survivor…that comes from *somewhere*. That's why you could survive, finish what you started."

That's why boxers train so intensely, not just to minimize the chance of getting hurt in the ring through physical conditioning, but so they can *finish* what they started. One time, when Coach said these words, I was doing upper-body training drills up a flight of stairs, walking on my hands. A lightweight boxer stood behind me, lifting my feet off the ground to force all my upper body weight onto my arms. At the top of the stairs stood a handful of fighters struggling to catch their breath after undergoing the same drill. It was hard. *But I finished.* I finished again during a drill to strengthen my legs, when I carried a boy boxer piggyback up the stairs.

"Damn!" a fighter exclaimed when I reached the top. "I've never seen a girl do that before!"

Working with Coach made me realize how strong my mind and body were becoming, and my dreams of championship titles were within reach. I contemplated these thoughts as sweat still dripped from my forehead after that exhausting workout, and Coach gave me a swig of water. He then said something I found insightful yet eerie, as though he knew my darkest secrets, the part of me I wanted to forget.

"In this sport, all the fears you've ever had will come out. Even from the time you were a little girl."

His words made me remember a time of suffering, a time I didn't think I'd survive. I thought I left those demons behind—my dad's violent side, my parents' volatile divorce, the fear of watching my mom struggle as a single mother of three, the insecurity that manifested when I was obese as a kid. How could boxing raise those fears again? Coach's words brought back confusion and pain that I spent most of my life trying to leave behind. Then, he switched gears.

"You're fighting again soon. It's only eight weeks away, the National Blue and Gold. It's the first time this competition has been open to females. Women from all over the U.S. are coming to fight."

"Will I be ready in time?"

"Yes."

"How good are these women boxers?"

"Not as good as you."

THE MOVE UP from exhibition fighter to national amateur contender came as fast as that—two months. This time it was a real match, with the outcome on my permanent boxing record. I trained like hell starting eight weeks out, and the closer it came to fight time, it was only going to get harder. I had a dream shortly after I agreed to compete in the National Blue & Gold. I saw the other female boxers, eight of them, none as fit and trim and ready to fight as I was.

Back to reality, Coach's nephew, Deon, another veteran boxer, was preparing me for the tournament, slated for September 5 at Baldwin Park in Los Angeles. The year was 1998, and at that time, female boxers were still a tiny niche. Everything about the boxing matches was designed for males, from the boys' boxing shorts that girls had to wear, to the plastic trophies topped with boy figures that the girls took home after a win.

Deon, Coach's protégé, was much like his uncle, with the same stoic presence, his ebony skin stretched tight over every muscle. His voice was deep and intimidating, but as tough as he was as my trainer, he was encouraging and always respectful, never objectifying me as a woman. Like his uncle's, Deon's words of wisdom fueled my spirit as much as my athleticism.

"You don't want to be just good. There are plenty of good fighters. You want to be the best. That means the hard work never ends in this sport. No matter how much you learn, there's always more to learn."

"I never knew how hard it would be until I committed myself one hundred percent. Training is so hard, sometimes I feel nauseous. Sometimes, I feel like I'm gonna pass out."

"That's a good sign. It means you're pushing yourself to the limit."

"Seriously? Feeling faint from a workout is a *good* sign?"

"You haven't passed out yet."

"Deon, my back hurts. My hands ache. My knuckles are skinned and bloody. I always have a headache 'cause I'm starving to make weight. My legs are always sore."

"But you love it..."

I couldn't help but laugh. "Yes. More than anything."

"I get it."

"I love it. And I hate it. I think about quitting all the time. But then I come back for more."

All the hard work, months of pain, what would it all be for if I quit? Whenever I felt like giving up, something inside told me to keep going. It was almost as though the journey itself was intended to teach me so much more. Boxing gave me courage. Boxing built my self-esteem. Boxing taught me I could do things I never dreamed I could do before. Boxing made my body and my mind strong. And perhaps most important: boxing gave me an outlet for my masked insecurity, my hidden rage, the anger I kept hidden from everyone who knew me. The ring provided a legal arena for me to lash out. The roped-off square was my sanctuary, my salvation, a space where my rage was embraced.

"In the ring, you have to want to hurt the other person because they want to hurt you," Deon once told me. "They're in your house. They're in your territory. It's gang warfare."

While training for the National Blue & Gold, my mind was focused on the fight when Coach surprised me: He wanted me to box in another exhibition just two weeks before. At first, I thought the matches were way too close.

"Coach, what if I get knocked out? If I get hurt, I'll have to pull out of nationals."

"You won't get knocked out. You won't get hurt."

"How do you know?"

"Because I know. You're a different fighter than you were with Layla. You're stronger now. Faster now. You have more endurance. You'll be fine. Trust me. Trust yourself."

"Okay...," I said with reluctance. "Will you be working my corner?"

"I can't. I'll be outta town. But Deon will be there. He'll take care of you. Meanwhile, keep trainin'. Hard."

When I trained, I often prayed for each session to end. I prayed for Deon to give me a water break. I prayed to hear him say, "Take a rest." The philosophy behind the training is to make the workouts so grueling, the actual fight seems easy. When you think you're going to die during training, and realize your body is much stronger than you thought, it's a good sign. Training is also about creating muscle memory. The more I perfected my jab, upper cut and straight right punch, the more natural these movements flowed in battle. The fight itself goes by quickly, with two minutes each round for a boxer to outpoint the other, or cut the fight short with a knockout. These 120 seconds are a flurry. The punches must flow without thought.

Training or torture? Before my formal two-hour workout in the boxing gym, I was already exhausted from running four miles with Deon on a high school track. Then I sparred four rounds with the guys during sessions that felt like a real match. When I thought I had nothing left in me, I skipped rope for half an hour, hit the heavy bag and speed bag for six rounds, and hit the focus mitts for five rounds. I shadow boxed for five rounds for footwork, and did 200 sit-ups for core strength.

Because of all this, I was in great shape the day my second exhibition arrived, August 29, 1998, at the Hilton Warner Center in Woodland Hills, on the western edge of the San Fernando Valley. When I was a little girl in the 1970s, only bean fields lined those streets. Now there was a luxury hotel, fancy restaurants and office towers—and me, a woman boxer. I didn't know who my opponent was, but I slept well the night before, with no doubts, no apprehension. Before my last exhibition, I was a bundle of raw nerves, but it was different this time. When Deon called me that morning, he further boosted my solidified confidence.

"Good mornin', champ. How ya feelin'?"

"Wired. Excited. A little scared. But excited."

"You're gonna do great. Get ready. I'm comin' to get ya. We gotta go to weigh-ins. You've lost more weight. It'll be no problem at the scale."

When we arrived at the Hilton, my competitor didn't show. I heard she was working, and would be there later that evening, less than an hour before we were to step into the ring.

"I want to see her," I told Deon. "What if she's a beast?"

Deon reassured me. "There's no way she's trainin' as hard as you. No way she's conditioned like you. You look like you just got outta boot camp. You've put in so much work. So much discipline. So much sacrifice. This fight will validate all the hours you put in the gym. You're gonna win tonight."

"Yes. I think so."

"No. You *know* so."

I told him about my dream of seeing eight female boxers at the National Blue & Gold. My premonition was odd, because Coach informed me a short time later that eight girls were signed up to fight. But with the nationals still two weeks away, I focused on the task before me: my second exhibition on a pro card commencing prior to the men's boxing matches. Hours before the fights began, I explored the ring, erected underneath towers of professional stage lights.

"Check it out—there's a camera," Deon pointed out. "This fight'll be televised."

It was summertime, with triple-digit temperatures I hoped would cool before I went toe-to-toe for three two-minute rounds.

"Damn. It's hot. I've never fought in this kind of heat."

"You've trained in this heat," Deon reminded me. "You're ready."

At Benny's, the air conditioning was never on, even in the summertime when the San Fernando Valley cooked in the scorching sun, creating a sauna-like space, locking all the body heat of the fighters training inside. My body acclimated to training in the heat, which would translate to fighting my exhibition that night, where the fight was staged outdoors on an elevated ring, and the surrounding concrete high-rises made it feel like an oven.

By 5 p.m., the temperature at 101 degrees, my competitor still hadn't shown. Typically when this happens, the match is canceled, and part of me felt relief at the possibility I wouldn't have to fight. But at 5:45 p.m., one of the boxing promoters told me my opponent had arrived. I went to the locker room to see the girl, who was a foot taller than me, giving her an advantage with a longer reach. But she was soft in the middle, with little definition in her arms, making me think she wasn't training half as hard as I was. Still, I learned to *never* underestimate an opponent: Layla wasn't ripped like me, and she kicked my ass. My competitor for this exhibition might not have looked in shape, but that didn't mean she wouldn't knock me out.

When I stepped on the scale earlier that day, I weighed in at 134. When the commissioner saw the weight of my opponent, 147 pounds, he didn't want the fight to go on.

"A thirteen-pound difference is too dangerous," the commissioner told Deon. "Alicia could get hurt."

Deon was confident in my ability.

"My girl's in shape. She's in great condition. She's ready to fight."

The commissioner turned to me to see my reaction.

"She's got thirteen pounds on you. Doesn't that concern you?"

"No," I replied, with Deon giving a nod of approval.

The fight was on. I learned the referee was a pioneer, too. Gwen Adair, professional boxing's only female ref and the first woman to referee a world title fight, a former actress who showed a dedication to the sport that earned her induction into the World Boxing Hall of Fame. Seeing Gwen in the ring felt like confirmation I was meant to be there, too. She came into the world of boxing long before me. She had already earned a place of respect as a woman in this male-dominated realm.

It was 103 degrees when my opponent and I stepped into the square. The crowd went wild with excitement at the chance to see two girls box.

"Girl fighters!" a woman sitting ringside screamed.

"Awesome!" yelled another. "Go girls!"

Some men in attendance weren't supportive.

"What a joke!" one man bellowed. "I wanna see 'em fight topless! Take it off!"

My opponent and I ignored the razz as we stood in the middle of the ring, staring intently into each other's eyes, with Gwen giving us instructions. In that moment, the realization of what I agreed to was almost paralyzing. Here I was again, about to enter battle, but this time, I was fighting a giant. Standing face-to-face with this girl, looking *up* at her, I thought, *Fuck! I made a mistake!*

I walked back to my corner to wait for the starting bell. Deon had only a few seconds to give me a shot of confidence.

"You got this!"

In the first round, I came out like a beast, the first to punch with my devastating left jab to her nose. She counterpunched quick, and surprise to me, her fists didn't inflict the hurt I felt from Layla. My confidence soared, forcing me forward, outpunching her three to one within the first thirty seconds of the fight. In the wake of my power, she stepped back, making me feel invincible, thrusting me forward to punch her again. Each time she tried to get away and counterpunch, I cut her off, outwitting her strategy, racking up points with my jab, which I had perfected while training by throwing hundreds each session until I felt like my arm was going to fall off. My jab alone dominated the fight. She got in a few good shots, but they felt like baby slaps compared to the punishment I endured with Layla and all the guys I trained with at Benny's. Round one was over. I went back to my corner, and from across the ring, I saw my opponent losing steam.

"You're doin' great!" Deon said with excitement, as though he was in the fight himself.

I didn't take my eyes off my opponent across the ring, heaving in her corner, her coaches wiping sweat from her arms and face, giving her water.

"Holy shit!" exclaimed a woman in the crowd. "These girls are awesome!"

"More! More! More!" yelled the man who taunted us in the beginning.

Entering round two, the adrenaline pulsing through my body felt like the greatest rush on earth, a natural high I never experienced in my life. This fight felt like a dream, like I was on cloud nine, outboxing a girl so much bigger than me. I felt like David battling Goliath, outsmarting the giant, knowing before the round was over I had already prevailed. Every time I threw my left jab, I connected and earned points, so I kept it going, followed up with my hard right each time I saw an opening. By the end of round two, I knew I had her beat.

"One round left," Deon said in my corner, his smile beaming, knowing he prepared me for this fight, like a father who prepared a child to enter the harsh world. "Keep doin' what you're doin'. Keep up that jab—all day long."

When the bell for the third round tolled, the crowd was on its feet, cheering for us girls who gave them a show they never expected. When men box, there are lulls in the rounds, with men taking brief moments to think on their feet as they strategize their combinations to outwit their opponent. But when women box, the punches don't stop, the flurry doesn't end until that bell rings—or the ref steps in to stop the fight.

During the last round, even though my opponent was spent, she kept on punching, like she was fighting for her life. Despite her visible fatigue, and no power behind her blows, she fought like an injured lioness protecting her precious cubs. When the final bell rang ending the fight, we embraced in sportsmanship as fellow athletes. Our arms wrapped around each other's sweat-covered bodies, heaving to catch our breath.

"You did great!" I told her.

She smiled, with a look of relief the battle was over.

"You're little. I thought this'd be an easy fight. I was wrong."

Gwen gently pulled us apart, stood between us, and raised both our arms as winners.

"Let's hear it for these ladies!" she commanded, and the crowd roared.

Stepping out of that ring, the feeling I felt was so grand, I didn't want it to end. I wished I could somehow bottle the emotions up, save them for later, and drink my victory at will. In those moments, I had no doubt, no fear, no insecurity. I felt beautiful, powerful and in control, like nobody could touch me, nobody could hurt me, that I'd never be afraid of anything again.

Me with boxing referee Gwen Adair after my exhibition match in 1998 at the Hilton Warner Center in Woodland Hills.

5 FIRST FIGHT

"Losers are winners who quit, even if you lose, you still win if you don't quit."—Cus D'Amato

Twenty-four hours before the National Blue & Gold tournament, all the boxers showed up for weigh-ins at the recreation center in Baldwin Park, Los Angeles. I came in at 129 pounds, lighter than the cut-off for my weight class of 132. I busted my ass to get as lean as I could, and all that hard work reflected at the scale. Deon and Coach, who were working my corner, praised my dedication.

"Good job comin' in lighter," Deon said.

"Thanks. But I'm *staaarving*," I said, laughing. Up to that point, my daily diet consisted of three egg whites, one grapefruit, one skinless white chicken breast, two apples and two cups of broccoli, and occasionally, only when I felt light-headed, eight raw almonds.

"It's part of the discipline of boxing," Coach said. "We'll go out for a big steak after you fight."

Our conversation stopped when an official with USA Boxing announced the matches between the girl fighters were made. All our names were written on a giant poster board taped to a concrete wall, where a crowd of girl fighters and their coaches swarmed to see who was paired for one-on-one battle. When I saw the name of my competitor, my heart sank. It was Layla, the same girl who kicked my ass at the Boys & Girls Club during my first exhibition match. Coach's wife, Cathy, whom I befriended in all the months I spent with her husband at the boxing gym, approached me to say what I already knew.

"You'll be fighting the same girl you fought the first time," she said, matter-of-factly. "Piece of cake."

Piece of cake my ass, I thought. That fight was *hard.* I had just experienced my greatest high in boxing when I beat the giant at my second exhibition. I wanted to hold onto the feeling of being on cloud nine. But the moment I saw Layla's name next to mine, I fell off that cloud into a black hole of fear, uncertainty and insecurity. The feeling of elation I wanted to possess forever instantly disappeared. Coach saw the terrified look on my face and knew what I was thinking. He cupped my cheeks with his hands and turned my gaze away from the names on the poster board.

"You're remembering that first experience. That's all in the past. Stay in the present. You're here now. You're ten times better now."

"Ten times better? Maybe. But am I good enough to fight Layla again? If I'm better, she's better. I don't want another standing eight, Coach. I don't wanna get knocked out."

"You *won't* get knocked out, trust me. You still don't realize how good you've become, how good you are."

Coach's words gave no comfort. All I could think about was how strong Layla was, how bad her punches hurt, her ownership of the ring.

"Of *all* people, why do I have to fight *her* again?"

"You know why. There aren't many girl boxers out there. This is a national tournament. This year, it's open to girls. Where else are they gonna fight?"

I knew I had trained hard. I knew I was in shape. And I tried to muster a bit of confidence, despite the level of my fear, knowing I couldn't be defeated mentally before I stepped in the ring. When I first fought Layla, I didn't know what the hell I was doing, and I survived. Even though she had nine fights under her belt and I had zero experience, I survived.

Coach knew I was overthinking.

"Stop worrying. You're meant to be here. You gotta have faith in yourself. You gotta trust yourself. You're a different fighter now, a better fighter now."

Later that evening, alone at home, I broke down. A wave of past experiences washed over me, things I rarely spoke of, traumas I locked away deep in my soul, dark memories I believed were powerless. I thought boxing was the cure to silence the demons in my head, but I was wrong. Coach was right: boxing brings up all fears. Now, I understood what he meant, but this time, his words fulfilled a deeper meaning of metaphor. Boxing brings up fears for you to face head on, like facing an opponent in the ring. In boxing, as in life, there's nowhere to run and hide, the only way out is through. For years, I avoided the *through* part. I never wanted to go through remembering those experiences again. Merely thinking about them gave them life, like they happened yesterday.

My negativity spiraled downward, sucking me into an emotional black hole, making me question every choice I had made. I never felt so alone, and I didn't know where these feelings were coming from. And why now, when I had to fight Layla in a matter of hours? What was I supposed to learn from this? Backing out of the fight wasn't an option—I worked too hard to get there. I tried to switch my mindset to have complete and total faith. But I needed help. So I hopped in my car and drove to Kid Gloves. It was late, around closing time at the gym, and I prayed Robert was there.

"What are you doing here?" Robert asked the moment I walked in the door. "Aren't you fighting tomorrow?"

"Yes," I replied, my eyes filled with tears.

"What's wrong?"

"I'm fighting Layla again. *Layla*. Of all the girls in the nation, I'm fighting her again."

Robert knew why I was so upset. He was there the day I got a standing eight with Layla.

"Don't worry," he said, embracing me. "You're so much better now. You've trained hard for this fight. You're gonna do great."

"I'm so scared."

"It's normal to be scared. I'd be worried if you weren't. But you gotta step through that fear to get to the other side."

I WOKE UP the morning of tournament day with very little sleep. But soon I was at ringside, with the time in between a blur. Robert brought his family and several members of Kid Gloves to cheer me on. An up-and-coming amateur fighter, Debbie, was also there, and tied my hair in a tight French braid that fit nicely underneath my bulky headgear. The love and support I received overpowered the negativity I felt in the previous hours, giving me a bit of relief.

This is how movie stars must feel, I thought to myself as my fans swarmed around me.

Robert wrapped my hands in gauze and tape for the fight, preparing my fists for the twelve-ounce boxing gloves I'd wear. Because USA Boxing sanctioned this tournament, strict rules applied to the hand wraps: the use of any substance on the bandage is prohibited, and an authorized equipment inspector must approve the wraps, writing their signature directly on the bandage, so no boxer can claim foul play after the fight. The intensity of these rules, punctuated by the adoration of people surrounding me before the fight, filled my ego with a sense of elation, distracting my thoughts from the task at hand: stepping into the ring with Layla.

Robert Ortiz wraps my hands for my first amateur boxing match at the 1998 National Blue & Gold Championship tournament in Los Angeles.

Coach, watching me from a distance, knew my mind wasn't in the game. Without making eye contact with anyone but me, he walked up, took me by the hand, and pulled me away.

"You gotta come down to earth," he said sternly, guiding me into a nearby hallway, where he and Deon wanted privacy to speak with me one-on-one.

"Layla is ranked top in the nation," Coach emphasized. "You're a better fighter than before. But you still have to take this seriously. Yes, your fans love you. But save 'em for later. You have a few minutes before the fight. Go prepare."

Stan "Coach" Ward (far right) gives me a pep talk before my first amateur match at the 1998 National Blue & Gold tournament in Los Angeles. Pictured center is Deon Lyons, Stan's nephew who was my trainer and corner man.

One of the most excruciating aspects of boxing was waiting, sometimes worse than the fight itself. The thoughts of losing, getting knocked out or getting my nose busted were overwhelming and vivid as my mind flashed with worst-case scenarios. Unlike many boxers who watched other matches before they stepped into the ring, I was different. For my preparation, I found a quiet place to be alone with my thoughts to calm my mind as best I could. I followed Coach's orders and found an empty classroom at the recreation center, where I sat at a student's desk, put on my walkman, and listened to the same music I played during my roadwork. I started to get pumped listening to AC/DC's *Thunderstruck* and *Highway to Hell* as I visualized taking my opponent out. My concentration broke when I heard a man's voice on the loudspeaker: "Alicia Doyle. Layla McCarter. Ring one."

As I walked out of that classroom, where Coach and Deon waited to escort me to my corner, my heart raced when I saw Coach carrying my towel and water bottle inside a bucket and Deon holding my black mouthpiece in his left hand. In a time span that felt like a few seconds, Layla and I were inside the ring in opposite corners, sitting on our stools, our coaches giving us last-minute instructions before the starting bell.

"Keep up your jab—all day long," Coach demanded.

"When you see an opening, hit 'er with your hard right," Deon instructed.

"And remember, you trained for this," Coach said. "You're not the same fighter you used to be."

With my gloves up to protect my face, I moved toward Layla in the center of the ring, where I was forced to be in the present and set aside what happened between us in the past. She was the first to punch, quickly scoring with a left-right-left combination, which I followed up with a triple-jab to her face.

"Good!" Coach yelled from my corner. "Hard right!"

I felt my body wind up. Starting with my left toe, energy moved up through my left leg into my core, surging inertia through my right arm, ending with an explosion through my right fist into Layla's face. She looked shocked, took a step back, and smiled at me through her mouthpiece, as though she was happy to be in the ring with a contender. She came forward again, throwing more combinations that hurt my face and body, but not nearly the same pain I felt during our first fight. And this time, I didn't back down. It was clear from the start she was racking up points and outscoring me in the first round, but I held my ground with my strong sturdy legs and never stepped backwards. I was determined to move forward no matter how much punishment she dished out.

"Jab! Jab! Jab!" Deon screamed.

"Hard right!" Coach bellowed.

The crowd at ringside was yelling in favor of both of us fighters. But I only deciphered the sounds of Coach and Deon, their voices etched in my ears through months of training, forcing a knee-jerk reaction of execution upon command. When round one was over, I was surprised at how fast the first 120 seconds flew by. I walked back for a thirty-second rest to my corner, where Coach bluntly stated the facts.

"She's winning. You gotta throw more punches. Throw more jabs. Score with your jabs."

Going into round two, I executed his strategy, but still got outpunched by Layla's quick combinations to my face and shots to my liver. Flustered, I hit her back, peppered her with jabs, but knew she was still outscoring me. At the end of round two, Coach encouraged me in the corner.

"She didn't see this coming. Your jab is working. Keep it up."

The bell rang for round three, and I was relieved I only had 120 seconds to go. I knew knocking Layla out was my only chance to win, and looked for openings to hit her with my hard right. This worked, and I connected, but my power shots failed to slow her down, and gave her openings to sock me in the right side of my body with her left upper cuts. When the final round ended, I knew I had lost, but I was also relieved knowing our second fight was nothing like the first. This time, her punches inflicted pain, but I was able to endure the punishment better. Because I survived so many whacks to the face and body while sparring with the guys, innately I knew the level of punishment my body could take. I was able to focus more on bobbing, weaving and slipping Layla's punches, and counterpunching in the brief moments she missed or stopped. I was pleased to get in a few good shots, push Layla back, and see the look on her face at the new fighter I had become.

Our fight went to the scorecards in the end, and I lost by a few points. I knew I wasn't winning early on, but when the referee raised Layla's hand in victory instead of mine, my head fell in shame. I lost *again* to Layla, and this time, the score went on my permanent record in amateur boxing, signified with a checkmark in the square box next to the letter L in my boxing passbook.

But the winner and loser didn't seem to matter much to the crowd of people who came to cheer us on.

"Great fight!" one of Layla's fans said to me when I climbed out of the ring.

"Badass!" said another, who asked for my autograph.

Coach and Deon gave praise, too.

"You held your ground," Coach told me. "You never backed down, not once. No matter what she threw at you, you kept movin' forward."

"I *knew* you had it in you," Deon commended. "I know you were scared goin' into this fight. And you still got in there. You walked through your fear. Faced it head-on."

I knew my cornermen were right, but their words failed to comfort me.

"I still lost."

Robert was nearby when I said those three words.

"You're looking at it all wrong. When you can pick yourself up in defeat, you're a winner."

As bad as I felt, I had to look at the bright side. Layla didn't cost me another standing eight, and the pain she inflicted wasn't half as bad as the first time. Was I getting used to it? Still, yet again, I thought about quitting boxing all together. I lost in front of all my friends. I was beat in front of an audience. I was mired in the thoughts of my defeat when Layla approached me after our match. It was the first time I heard her speak, the first time I stood in her presence without the threat of a fight.

"You did great. That was a good fight."

Then she hugged me—that's how advanced her level of sportsmanship was.

"I don't *ever* want to box you again," I told her. "Please go pro so I never have to fight you again in amateurs."

Two days after the National Blue & Gold, Coach wanted me to fight again in two weeks. But my ego remained bruised from losing my first amateur fight. I told him I wasn't ready. I needed more time.

"Alicia, when you go to a job interview and you don't get the job, do you stop looking?"

"No. But I have so many doubts."

"In this sport, all the fears you've ever had will come out. But when you fall down, you gotta pick yourself up. You have to have faith in yourself. Just because you didn't win doesn't mean you lost. You grew emotionally in that fight."

In the following days, the sting of my loss grew worse, and less than two weeks after my first amateur fight, I backed out of my second. I showed up at the gym in plain clothes without my boxing gear. I had already made up an excuse for why I couldn't compete, that I was scheduled to work, which was a lie. The fear of losing again was just too much, but I also realized the further I went in boxing, the deeper I had to dig emotionally, which meant remembering a past I wanted to leave behind. Boxing brought up my insecurities from childhood. Moving forward in the sport meant bringing up these memories again and facing them head on.

"You're late," Coach said when I walked in the door. "What's wrong? You're never late."

"I know…I'm sorry, Coach."

"We're gettin' ready to spar. Where's your gear? You have a fight in two weeks."

"I can't fight in that match. I have to work."

I felt horrible lying to Coach, who saw right through me. His response echoed across the gym, where men I sparred with heard the deliberation behind his words.

"Now I have to call those people and tell them my girl chickened out!"

Damn, that's embarrassing, I thought to myself. But I also knew Coach didn't intend to humiliate me.

"I know you're lying, but that's okay. You're trying to figure stuff out. We've all been there. This is the toughest sport in the world. Just know, we're all here for you. And we *still* love you."

"Sometimes, I don't know why I'm here. I don't know why I'm doing this. I don't know what I'm trying to prove. That loss was so hard. I can't get it out of my head."

"You have to turn the page. Tomorrow is another day. This will become whatever you make it. The greater you believe you are, the greater you'll be."

6 GENESIS OF RAGE

"Most people aren't good or bad. They're naive."
—Jake LaMotta

Why would a woman box? From the time I started boxing in the late 1990s, and even after I retired from the sport, people ask me this question. I never give a clear response, because the answer is too deep, perhaps too disturbing, and would take too long to explain in short sound bites. One might think I boxed for the fame and bragging rights that align with being one of few women boxers in the United States. I admit, those reasons were alluring at times, especially with the extensive press coverage and adoration from fans I received. But my reasons for stepping in the ring came from a much more primal place, starting with the anger and violence I witnessed and experienced as a child, insidiously evolving into my own rage that took my lifetime to decipher and transcend. To understand this evolution, it's important for me to convey the pieces of circumstance, and the sum of all parts, that led me to immerse myself in one of the most brutal sports known to man. The short explanation is that I was raised in an atmosphere of volatility, too young to understand the nature of these occurrences until I became an adult. The longer explanation starts with my parents—whom I love and respect for their vulnerability and fallibility—and for giving me the opportunity to bear witness to their complex humanness, struggles and heartbreak.

Why would a woman box? By sharing these pieces of myself, starting from the beginning, my hope is that those asking the question will have what I consider a simple answer: No wonder.

HOW DID MY PARENTS MEET? Among the many versions of the story, one point remains consistent: My mom was "a real looker." And the moment my dad laid eyes on her, he was hooked.

My mom, born in 1934, is the daughter of immigrants who came to America from China and settled in Arizona in the early 1900s. In Chinese families, the desired firstborn is a son—a sign of good luck. But my mom, being born first, grew up in the shadow of her brother, who was born second, followed by two younger sisters. My mom was expected to be seen and not heard, typical of Chinese views toward women in the 1930s. She was pretty, making her ideal for marriage and making babies. She followed the societal rules, as there were few choices for women back then, leaving them limited options as teachers, secretaries and librarians. Under this oppression, she left her home in Arizona at age sixteen, attempting to escape the rules of the time. She hopped into her Volkswagen bug and drove to Southern California, where a friend helped her land a job at a department store. She worked there for many years, trying to make her way in the world, attempting to forge a new reality, a construct contradicting the expectations of women at the time.

These ideals faded away when she was sucked back into the societal matrix, marrying the first time to a Chinese man. They had two sons, my future half-brothers, Luke and Matthew. The boys were little when their father became ill and underwent brain surgery, and afterwards walked with a slight limp and spoke with a slur. My mom, believing she'd be stronger on her own raising two boys, dissolved the marriage. Soon after, my dad came into the picture.

My dad is from Hungarian roots, with a splash of Cheyenne Indian from his grandmother of six generations ago, who made the pioneer trek across the American plains, a covered-wagon convoy that led to the death of several of my ancestors. Their original last name was Smith, changed to Doyle by dad's grandfather six generations back, because only the Irish were being hired as laborers back then. My great-great-great-great grandpa, knowing work was his only way of survival, took the last name Doyle, which belonged to one of the most powerful families in Ireland at the time.

My dad was born the oldest of three with two little sisters into a poor family. The little money his parents acquired was spent on booze, fueling my grandparents' alcoholism and neglect of their children, whom they sometimes left behind in the car while my grandparents were at the bar drinking. My father's father had a violent side and abused my dad in unimaginable ways, like the time my dad was eight and my grandpa threw him down a flight of stairs. My dad's physical survival masked an imprint—an invisible scar of insecurity and never believing he was good enough—that remained for his lifetime, causing a chain reaction of things to come. Grandpa never abused his daughters, creating more confusion for my dad, forcing him into mental reclusiveness as an escape. Dad's mind was his greatest weapon, and his brilliance led to an engineering career working on classified missions. One of my father's greatest feats occurred when the Doyle name was affixed to the Cassini probe, a spacecraft that studied the planet Saturn, its rings and moons.

In my dad's first marriage, he had three children—a daughter and two sons. When he met my mom, he was still married to his first wife, who my mom didn't know existed. My mom and dad spent as much time together as they could, except on the days when my dad went MIA. My mom trusted he was working, and never considered he hid the façade of fulfilling obligations with his first family. My mom was immersed in her love for my dad until she heard from an acquaintance that he lived a double life. She gathered up my dad's belongings in their shared space, threw them outside on the front lawn, and vowed to never see him again. But my dad wanted my mom back, divorced his first wife and left his family, making new promises to my mother in matrimony. Their new blended family relocated to the San Fernando Valley in Southern California when I was born in 1970, but the following year, the big earthquake of 1971 hit hard, measuring 6.5 on the Richter scale. The devastation led to our move to Colorado, where we settled in Wheatridge, a suburban town where snow-filled winters froze a nearby lake for ice skating, and rain-filled springs turned the aspen trees gold and red. We lived in a single-story home on a quiet cul-de-sac walking distance from my elementary school, and in this small town, I felt safe walking three blocks to campus, carrying my metal Holly Hobbie lunchbox.

For a few years, we seemed like a picture-perfect family: My parents, the beautiful young couple, with two little Chinese boys from my mom's first marriage. When I was born, Luke and Matthew gave me the nickname Toy, because, as they put it, "she looks like a toy." I lucked out with genetics, with a beautiful Chinese mom, and a handsome dad with strong Native American Indian cheekbones. We were the cutest family on the block, where we kids rode bicycles and played hide-and-seek with the neighborhood children.

But the passion between my parents flipped upside down early on, their pasts bubbling to the surface, coming to a boiling point they didn't have the emotional tools to mitigate. Before they wed, they rarely if ever discussed the painful details of their histories. I often wondered years later if their marriage would have lasted if they had communicated and revealed their vulnerabilities—exposed their deepest heartaches and the darkest parts of themselves—in a space of love and trust.

Soon after we moved to Colorado, when I was in kindergarten, their fighting began. My mom believed my dad was being unfaithful. He would lock himself in his den in our home, where he spent hours talking on the phone with *someone*, emerging from this space visibly disturbed from the conversation that transpired. My dad didn't divulge the truth: he was talking with his mother about his father, trying to work through the abuse my dad endured as a boy, trying to make sense of it all. Yes, my dad survived and became what many consider a rocket scientist, and rebuilt a second family of his own. But the emotional scars from his childhood remained unresolved. No matter how old we are, no matter how much we accomplish in life, the broken parts of ourselves remain etched in our psyches.

Their fights lasted for hours behind closed doors in their bedroom. Within earshot, in my bedroom, I hid in the corner of my closet behind my long dresses, clutching my stuffed animals, crying and shaking, too young to make sense of the reasons behind their quarrels. Luke and Matthew were great big brothers to me during these times, luring me away from my hiding space to play games in a room downstairs in our basement, where they refocused my attention to jigsaw puzzles and coloring books. My parents fought so often, I became desensitized to their spats, which escalated to the point of ridiculousness. Like the time we were sitting around the table at dinner, and my dad threw a plate of food against the wall, smashing the porcelain to bits, leaving green Jell-O stuck to the paint. Or the time he retreated to our basement and smashed plates packed inside a cardboard storage box with a sledgehammer, leaving a mangled pile of broken glass.

I witnessed my first act of violence at five years old when their verbal abuse turned physical. To this day, I don't know what my mom and dad were fighting about, but the violence remains etched in my memory. My dad grabbed my mother by the neck with both hands, shoved her against the wall, and lifted her to her toes. Their eyes locked in shock. Time stopped to a deafening silence, and from there, unfolded in slow motion. My mom closed her eyes, her arms fell limp to her sides, and my dad released her, with a look of horror on his face, stunned at what he had done. I sat on the floor in my pink nightgown, looking up at them, crying uncontrollably and babbling nonsense only a child that young could express. The two people I loved more than anything on earth were ripping each other apart, shattering my world.

I hyperventilated through my wails. My dad looked down at me, his eyes streaming with tears, the sight of which made me more afraid than I'd been in my life up to that point. I never saw my dad cry before—or any grown man, for that matter—which made me shake with fear of the unknown and of what would happen next. My dad saw the pain he caused us both, turned away and headed for our garage door to leave.

I wrapped my little body around his right leg in an attempt to keep him there.

"Don't leave, Daddy! Please…please…please don't leave, Daddy!"

He tried to shake me loose, but I wouldn't let go, clinging tight.

"I'm no good, I'm no good," he said as he heaved from emotional and physical exhaustion.

"Let him go!" my mom commanded.

I released my grip, and crawled on my hands and knees as fast as I could to our garage door.

"Don't leave!" I screamed, trying to block his exit.

"I have to leave, baby girl," he said, gently pushing me to the side. "Just remember, I love you."

My father Frank Doyle and I feeding birds when I was a toddler.

7

ORIGIN OF INSECURITY

"You don't lose if you get knocked down. You lose if you stay down."—Muhammad Ali

Each moment of our lives is a piece of us and part of a puzzle—pieces of pain, joy and heartbreak—pieces that make us question whether to go on, pieces we'd rather throw away. The heartbreak pieces are hardest to assemble, but those are the ones that make us who we are. And once we fit these painful pieces into the bigger picture, we see the beautifully complex mosaic of our life.

I started collecting my heartbreak pieces as a child, and never knew how they'd fit together, what my bigger picture would look like or how this mosaic would leave a space for boxing, a void to be filled with blood, sweat and tears. Looking back, I realize the heartbreak pieces were necessary to fuel my grit in the ring—where I ultimately found my salvation.

My dad's departure shattered my world, like dropping a box full of puzzle pieces down a flight of stairs, some falling into empty crevices, never to be found again, leaving the puzzle unfinished. When my dad left, I was too young to comprehend the magnitude of this void. It sounds cliché to say God had a greater plan for me, but I believe this is true. I didn't come into the world to have a picture-perfect early life, and I believe everything I went through prepared me for two of my life's greatest accomplishments: becoming a journalist and becoming a champion in the boxing ring.

Before my parents' divorce, my dad often wrote his thoughts on pieces of paper, which he tacked to the cork bulletin board in his den. One passage in particular I was too young to understand, but today, his words hold deep meaning:

> Life is a series of goals or projects that inspire and fulfill us; but there are down times. Vacuums in our psyche that occur when we pass through the inevitable disenchantment with our current life's course. This is normal, and not to be concerned about.

I was in the first grade when my parents separated. My dad moved to an apartment near Denver, about an hour away from Wheatridge, where I saw him every other weekend. The psychological effect of my parents' separation hit me hard, and manifested into sleepwalking spells where I left my house and wandered around our cul-de-sac. My only memory of this was one time, in the middle of the night, when I walked to our neighbor's house next door. I knocked and the couple answered, surprised by the confused little girl in her pink nightgown and bare feet.

"Toy? What are you doing here?

"I'm *scaaared*, nobody's home."

At that moment, Luke arrived home and pulled into our driveway. He saw me right away, and ran to my side.

"Looks like we have a little sleepwalker," he told our neighbors as he picked me up in his arms.

I don't remember my brother taking me back inside or putting me back to bed. But the next morning, after fixing me a bowl of cereal for breakfast, he asked me about it.

"Do you remember what happened last night?"

I didn't understand the question.

"You left the house, Toy. Did you have a nightmare?"

For a moment, I thought I was in trouble.

"I don't remember."

The following few years of seeing my dad only two weekends a month took a toll on my spirit. I missed him horribly, and anxiously awaited these visits, counting every moment until I saw him again. Days before his arrival, I packed my pink suitcase in anticipation, and on Friday nights, I'd sit in front of our house on the sidewalk, watching for him to pull around the corner. But sometimes, he didn't show up, leaving me there for hours, until my mother or two brothers convinced me to come back inside. Then, for the next two weeks until I saw my dad again, my mother, Luke and Matthew consoled me whenever I went through crying spells or nightmares that shocked me awake.

But when my dad did show up, I was so happy to see him I forgot about the days in between. Our next seventy-two hours were all about fun, and we packed in as much as we possibly could. On Friday nights, we went to the theater to see a James Bond movie, and dad let me eat all the candy I wanted from the concession stand. Dad also introduced me to the television show *Wonder Woman*, starring Lynda Carter, who I never truly appreciated at the time as a woman of power and righteousness, a fighter and female role model. One summer, dad taught me how to swim, and from that point on, we swam at a nearby recreation center every time I came to visit. One winter, he taught me how to ski, leading to fun times on the slopes in Aspen, Vail and Breckenridge. He took me camping, too, and taught me how to catch a fish, cut it open and gut it, and cook it on the open fire. I enjoyed gutting a fish, and my dad loved watching me do it, knowing his little girl wasn't squeamish.

My weekends with dad went along this way for a year or so while he was living alone. Our routine changed when he met Patty, a nurse, at a square dance. Patty spotted my dad from across a crowded room, approached him and said two words about his Western attire: "Nice shirt." They instantly hit it off, and when things got more serious between them, I spent every other weekend with my dad and Patty at her apartment near Denver, where I loved swimming in her pool, going to the drive-in movies with them, and spending the night in her living room on the fold-out bed. Patty was an excellent seamstress, and sewed my school clothes by hand; she was also a great cook, and made banana bread and cherry chip cookies from scratch whenever I came to visit. Patty treated me like the daughter she never had, and eventually became my dad's third wife. I loved being part of this new family structure. My dad and Patty were happy, never spoke an unkind word to each other, never fought, and remained consistently affectionate. Being with them gave me a sense of stability I no longer felt at home with my mom, still single and struggling with three children to raise on her own.

The worst part of my weekends with dad was going home. I hated leaving, and my tears started flowing on Sunday morning, when I knew I'd be without his presence later that evening. I asked dad to stretch the day out as long as he could, but in the back of my mind, I was miserable knowing we had to part. When evening came, and it was time for me to go home, I'd beg dad to take the long way, to stop at every red light, and lied about needing to pee so he'd make pit stops. During the drive, we listened to songs on my dad's eight-track that made us both cry, like Elvis Presley's *Green, Green Grass of Home*.

When I was in the second grade, I left my childhood home with my mom and two brothers when we moved a few miles up the road to a duplex. My mom took a full-time job to support us single-handedly, and was rarely home on the weekdays, giving me free reign of our house as a latchkey kid who came home to an empty house, as my older brothers were busy in high school with extracurricular activities and sports. Charged with cleaning our home daily, I washed dishes, vacuumed and made the countertops spotless before doing my homework. I also was supposed to be taking care of myself, but wasn't at all prepared for that, caring little about my own hygiene habits, and eating anything and everything I wanted, as food was my greatest comfort. By the time I was in the third grade, I'd gained quite a bit of weight, making me fatter than all the kids in school. That's when the bullying began, with the boys trashing me with every epithet they could think of: "fat-so," "fat-ass," "tub-a-lard," "fat Eskimo." I stood out at school, not only for my obesity, but because I wore the same clothes day after day. I looked like Pig Pen, smelled unclean, and went for days with unwashed hair. My mangled appearance, especially my knotted tangled hair, angered my mom.

"If you don't take care of your hair, I'm gonna have it all whacked off!" she often threatened.

I tried to maintain my hygiene, and juggle the madness of my home and school routine, until the day my mom got fed up with my appearance.

"We're getting your hair cut," she said one day when she came home from work.

"Please don't," I pleaded. "I'll take care of it."

"It's a mess," she insisted. "You like Dorothy Hamill's hair. We'll make it look like hers."

That evening, I cried when I looked in the mirror, and dreaded going back to school, where for the next two weeks, I wore a hooded sweater to hide my embarrassment. The bullies taunted me even more, and because I dealt with the inner battle of my home life, I had no inner strength or self-esteem to fight back, making me an easy target. One of the biggest blows happened in sixth grade on Valentine's Day, when I looked forward to picking out Valentines for my classmates for our classroom party. My teacher organized a contest to see who could design the best Valentine's box, and the winner received a blue ribbon. I put all my energy into creating my special Valentine keeper out of a shoebox, which I wrapped in three layers of crepe paper, each in a different shade of purple. Once the glue dried, I cut a hole in the top so my classmates could slip their Valentine's cards inside. During the classroom party, the girls loved my box, and my teacher did, too, earning me the top prize. I had never won anything before and was elated to get my blue ribbon, but was knocked off my cloud when I opened my box to read an anonymous note:

"BLIMP WEIGHS 10,000000000 POUNDS!!!"

The only way I got through those grade school years was because of Ms. Pidgeon, the school psychologist, who my mom signed me up to see once a week starting in the second grade. This happened after one of our neighbors, the father of a girl around my age who lived a couple houses away, spoke to my mom about me.

"There's something wrong with Toy."

"Why would you say that? What are you talking about?"

"She's at our house after school when you're at work. She's way too sensitive. She cries all the time. Even when the kids are just joking and playing around like normal kids, Toy ends up crying."

"She's had a hard time since her father left. I can't be there for her like I wanna be. I'm a single mom raising three kids alone. I'm just trying to keep a roof over our heads. I'm barely making ends meet."

"I can't imagine how hard it must be for you."

"It wasn't supposed to be this way. We weren't meant to end up this way."

"I'm worried about your daughter, so I did some checking around. There's a school psychologist who helps kids from broken homes. Her name is Ms. Pidgeon. She can help Toy."

"Okay. I'll look into it. Thank you for looking out for my daughter. I know I'm not the best mom when it comes to her."

"You're doing the best you can. Toy will be okay."

My sessions with Ms. Pidgeon helped me feel safe at school, where she pulled me out of the classroom once a week for one hour, until I graduated from the sixth grade. I looked forward to Wednesdays at ten a.m., when Ms. Pidgeon took me to her counseling room on campus, where we never spoke about the dissension going on in my home life. In this space, I was happy just being a kid. My favorite activity was playing with a family of bendable plastic dolls—a mother, a father, two children and a baby—and I acted out scenarios with these figures having fun as the loving family I wanted. Ms. Pidgeon's kindness earned my trust through consistency and reliability, and the assurance that our time together was private. Our meetings lasted until I left elementary school for a new campus in junior high. Our sessions were like the steam release on a pressure cooker. Without them, who knows? I might've exploded.

Luke was also a comfort in my life. Despite what he experienced growing up—watching our mom go through two failed marriages and witnessing my father's abusive side—he possessed a level of calmness, like the eye of a tornado. He was kind, gentle and compassionate, and despite his popularity as the valedictorian in high school, made time for me when he could, taking me out for ice cream from time to time so we could be together one-on-one. Because he was several years older than me, he left home early, at age seventeen after earning a scholarship. I cried for days after he went off to college, missing him terribly, as he was the man of the house after my parents' separation.

Now there were three of us, my mother and I, and my other big brother, Matthew. He and I never discussed our traumatic past, but tried to move forward with living our lives the best we could. That's when the fighting between him and me began over shared chores and the fact that I ate too much. But underneath the surface was our own struggle to make sense of our broken home life. Being so young, with no coping mechanisms to address what we were going through as children of divorce, we acted out, expressed our inner turmoil in the only way we knew how. We had no family counseling, support or outlet to transcend what happened to us, so we lashed out at each other through screaming matches full of hate, because all we had was each other. Our mom was too busy and stressed out with worry to pay attention to us in the way we needed. Her biggest concern was survival, keeping food in our fridge and a roof over our heads, which she miraculously maintained as a single mom. It was impossible for my mom to be there for us one hundred percent emotionally, because she was literally spent, and had no space to manage children of divorce all on her own.

Even though Matthew and I fought a lot, he had my back when it mattered, and his demonstrative acts, though few and far between, showed me he cared. One weekend, when I was around ten years old, my mom was home mending her skirts for work. I was full of energy, wanting to play, driving her nuts.

"Go outside and play!" she ordered, assuming I'd run next door to hang with the neighborhood children.

Instead, a few neighborhood kids and I rode our bikes to a bubbling creek miles away, where we swam in our clothes until dusk, with no intention of coming home anytime soon. I was gone for six hours, and when the sun started to go down, my mom panicked, as her house rules required me to be home went the street lights went on. She told my brother to bring me home, and he rode his bicycle all over the neighborhood until he found me. Our eyes locked, and I saw a sense of relief wash over him. But his mood changed quickly as he was overpowered with anger that I had disappeared for so long.

"You better get home," Matthew demanded. "You're in big trouble."

This defining moment reminded me that no matter how bad things were at home, no matter how bad we fought, he was my big brother, and had my back. And when he got accepted to college and moved out at age eighteen, leaving me alone with my mother, I knew he would be there for me when I needed him most.

Back at school, the bullies who tortured me during my elementary years were the same classmates I faced when I started junior high. A clique of popular boys got a kick out of humiliating me as a group, overpowering me with shame ten to one, giving each other high fives when they made me cry. The verbal abuse turned physical when I was walking through the school hallway to class, and a boy came toward me from the opposite direction. I put my head down to avoid eye contact, but he rushed toward me and slammed me into a concrete wall, making me drop my books and sending a surge of pain through the right side of my body. As I gathered up my books and started to cry, he screamed so loud his voice echoed through the hallway. "Get out of my way, you fat fucking bitch!"

The second attack happened in science class, where we sat in groups of five.

"Lay out your hand," demanded the boy sitting next to me. "I want to give you something."

"What?"

"Just do it!"

I reluctantly opened my palm. He stabbed me with a number two pencil, forcing a rush of blood mixed with black lead to the surface. He laughed uncontrollably, and pushed me so hard I fell out of my chair. The ruckus he caused made everyone in the classroom look our way as he yelled loud enough for everyone to hear: "You're such a stupid, fat, ugly bitch!"

8 SLEEPING PILLS

"To see a man beaten not by a better opponent but by himself is a tragedy."—Cus D'Amato

I was in junior high when my mom started dating again. We had already left our Methodist roots for the Mile Hi Church that she discovered in Lakewood, Colorado, where she met men through a singles group. The church's focus was called Science of Mind—established in the 1920s by Ernest Holmes—a spiritual, philosophical and metaphysical "religion" within the New Thought movement. *The Science of Mind* is also a book by Earnest Holmes. His writing details how people can actively engage their minds in creating change throughout their lives, with explanations of how to pray and meditate, heal oneself spiritually, and find self-confidence in what he describes as a philosophy and "a way of life." When I turned twelve, my mom enrolled me in classes for teens at this church, where we learned how to meditate and read each other's auras, and discussed the Science of Mind teachings with an advisor.

Through the church's singles group, my mom met the man who would become my stepfather. He seemed nice enough at first, attentive with my mom and benign with me, spending time at our house on the weekends. I knew they were growing closer when he started spending weeknights at our house, and I'd wake up in the morning to find him on our sofa, smoking cigarettes and watching television. I didn't know how serious my mom was about this man until she took me out to dinner one night. The invitation to spend time with her alone was a strange occurrence, because our relationship by that time was more strained than ever. When my parents were still married, my mom and I were as close as a mother and daughter could be. But after the divorce, my mom worked hard to support our family and came home from work exhausted all the time. This fueled fights between us the moment she walked in the door over chores I failed to complete, my increasing weight and poor grades, and my inability to hold my tongue when I disagreed with her. So when she picked me up after work to take me out to dinner, I was happier than I'd been in a long time. She let me choose the restaurant, Carl's Jr., where she said I could order anything I wanted.

Finally, I thought, I get to spend some fun one-on-one time with my mom. *Maybe we're getting back to the way we were.*

Then she said something that made my heart sink.

"When we get there, I have something to tell you."

"What?"

"Let's wait until we order dinner."

Carl's Jr. was crowded that night, and we sat at a table in the center of the restaurant, where I felt like the two of us were on display. I scarfed down my order of large fries before I asked her again.

"What do you have to tell me?"

"Well…you know I've been dating the same man for awhile."

"Yeah, the guy who smokes cigarettes and watches our TV. I can't watch my shows when he's there."

"Don't be a smart-ass."

"How am I being a smart-ass?"

"There you go again."

I shut up and ate the rest of my food in silence. Even though I was only twelve, I knew what was coming next, and I was mad she took me out to dinner in a crowded place to give me the news. I believed she planned it and knew I wouldn't approve. I felt betrayed.

"We're engaged. We wanna get married."

I looked down at my cheeseburger.

"Well, what do you think?"

I took a swig of my vanilla shake.

"Do you have *anything* to say?"

"What do you want me to say?"

"I'm *asking* how you feel. How you feel about us getting married."

"I don't know."

"You don't *know*?"

"I don't know, mom. I've got a bad feeling about him."

My mom looked enraged at my response.

"Well that's *too* bad. It's *my* turn now."

I thought to myself, *then why'd you ask me?* But I didn't dare say the words out loud. As a Chinese daughter of a Chinese mother, I was taught to be seen and not heard, and I learned over the years that talking back would get me slapped or grounded.

My opinion didn't matter, and soon enough, my mom and new stepdad got married during a one-week cruise, without my presence, and when they returned home, I was part of a new family. My mom was happy to be married again, but I felt disconnected from her, filled with emptiness, and at that point, wanted to die. I felt unloved, neglected and unsupported, still confused over my parents' divorce, and missed my dad more than ever. Visits with my dad became more infrequent, as my mother said horrible things about him to me, telling me he refused to pay child support, was a philanderer, and only cared about his new life with his new wife. This was far from the truth, I learned later on, but I didn't know any better, being only a kid, and not having the wisdom or resources to connect with my dad the way I wanted. I allowed the brainwashing to affect me, and before I knew it, grew distant from my father, not knowing his heart was breaking without my presence. Frustrated and depressed, with nobody to talk to, a toxic storm built inside me. The one thing I did know: I wanted my pain to end. So I planned my death the best I could. I wanted a painless suicide; I could not conceive of slitting my wrists, hanging myself, or drinking poison. I knew my mom took over-the-counter sleeping pills, so I started sneaking into the drawer where she kept them, collecting them one by one, and hiding them until I had a giant pile.

The day that I tried to kill myself, my mom and I fought worse than we ever had. I don't remember the exact details of what we were fighting over, only the hateful words that came out of our mouths.

"I *hate* you!" I screamed.

"I don't like you very much right now, either!" she yelled back.

I stormed into my bedroom and slammed the door, and my mom left our house to meet a friend for a few hours. During that time, I grabbed the sleeping pills, twenty tiny blue things, and looked down at them in the palm of my hand. I cried at the thought of what I was about to do, but felt no ounce of hope. I had nothing to live for. I believed nobody loved me, and that I was a nuisance to my mom in her new marriage. Sitting on the side of my bed, I popped the whole pile of pills in my mouth and took a swig of water. I didn't know at the time that the pills would simply put me to sleep for a very long time. I was a fat kid, and looking back, that's probably why I didn't die; being fat saved my life.

During the few hours my mother was gone, I think she contemplated our fight, or talked to her friend for advice, because when she came home, she showed kindness. She came into my room, sat on the side of my bed, and shook me gently to wake me up. I managed to open my eyes, surprised I was still alive.

"Are you up?"

I heard her voice, but the grogginess made opening my eyes difficult.

"I'm here."

I don't remember all the words my mom spoke. But I knew by the tone of her voice she apologized.

"You're my daughter. I love you, no matter what."

"I love you too, Mom."

I went back to sleep for many hours, and she never questioned why I slept for so long. By the time she returned to check on me the next morning, the sleeping pills had worn off, and we both acted like nothing had happened.

Two days later, I wrote my aunt in Arizona a letter about my attempted suicide and asked for guidance, hoped for a kind word, *anything* that would help me feel better. I thought my aunt would keep the letter private, but she shared it, leaking the news back to my mom. And when she found out, she was livid.

"I know what you did."

My faced flushed red with embarrassment and shame.

"I'm sorry, Mom..."

"Don't you think I want to kill myself every day? I'll have to hide my sleeping pills from now on."

I didn't think things could get any worse. Until later that week, when I went to get the mail, and saw that my aunt wrote me back. My heart dropped when I read her opening line.

"Honey, you have got to lose some weight."

Seriously? What does my weight have to do with me wanting

to kill myself? My pain held more weight than numbers on a scale. But my aunt's words stuck, and I thought, maybe she's right. That summer away from school, I cut my food intake by half, and rode my bike every day around a nearby lake in a circle of just over a mile. I rode until I felt my legs were going to give out, my stomach rumbling with hunger, with tears streaming down my face. Whenever I felt like binging, I looked through a book I assembled filled with photographs of skinny models I clipped from magazines. In three months, I lost thirty pounds, and returned back to school in the ninth grade with a brand new body. Word got around quickly with my classmates.

"Have you seen Alicia this year?"

"Yeah. She's not an ugly fat-ass anymore."

I stood in the assembly hall waiting for class to start when one of the most popular girls in my grade approached me. Ironically, she was a bit overweight herself. But she had a beautiful face, frosted blond hair, long eyelashes and big green eyes—and above all, exuded confidence.

"Everybody's talking about you."

Her presence intimidated me. I couldn't believe this popular girl was speaking to me after ignoring me for years at school.

"What about?"

"How skinny you are. I wanna know how you did it. I wanna be skinny too."

From that moment on, she and I were inseparable, connecting in between classes to banter, sitting together at lunchtime, and spending time together on the weekends, when I shared the details of how I lost thirty pounds. Because of her, I was in the popular clique, but this also added more confusion to my psyche. The bullying stopped, but I was the same person on the inside, with the same trauma and heartache, yet treated differently. Still, on some level, I felt happy, whatever *happy* means. For the first time, I felt normal. I fit in normal-sized clothes, I had friends like normal kids, and I finally had a boyfriend like normal girls. I didn't cry at school anymore. But this wouldn't last long. The summer after my freshman year ended, my mom announced we were returning to the place I was born.

"We're moving back to California."

She made the matter-of-fact statement out of the blue, with no room for my opinion or input, or how I felt about this huge change.

"Why?"

"I love California. I'm sick of the snow and cold winters. I've always wanted to go back."

"When?"

"Two weeks."

"Two weeks?" I started crying. "But all my friends are here. My boyfriend's here. My best friend's here. Dad's here."

"You'll adjust. You'll make new friends. And your dad…well, you two can write letters."

"I don't wanna go."

"That's too bad."

"What about my feelings?"

"What about your feelings? It's not about you."

9 FILLING THE VOID

"I've learned a lot about life besides how to take a punch. And I've taken quite a few in and out of the ring."—Jake LaMotta

It took three days to drive west from Colorado to the San Fernando Valley in California, where my mom's best friend had a guest house on her back lot. My mom and new stepdad moved into the back house, and I moved into the main house, where I shared a room with the daughter of my mom's friend. We were both about the same age, and I remember how generous she was, a fifteen-year-old like me, to share her room and make space in her closet for my stuff. I was a stranger inserted into this family's home, and they graciously tried to make my stay as comfortable as they could.

I started fall classes as a sophomore at Chatsworth High with more than 2,000 students, a huge change from my smaller campus environment in Colorado. Even though I wasn't the fat kid anymore, I worried I'd be teased again in this new world, for whatever reason. I also feared I'd be the only minority on campus, like I was in the lily-white suburbs where I grew up. When I walked into the classroom on the first day, I scanned the room for other minorities, and more than half the kids were Asian. With a student body that large, there was a clique for everyone—Goths, heshers, nerds, jocks, cheerleaders, chubby girls—and everyone in between. I joined the drill team, earning my place in the jock group, and met a boy named Bobby, my first love. He was popular and on the football team, so when I became his girlfriend, I was an instant social success story. We were known as the cute couple on campus, where I wore his football jersey on game days, and on the weekends, I was at his house, where I was adored by his big sister and parents.

About a year after my mom and stepdad and I moved to California, we moved out of the first place we landed into an apartment about five miles away from my high school. The dynamic in our home seemed okay at first, but it wasn't long before the friction between my stepdad and me grew problematic, which put an even bigger strain on the complicated relationship I had with my mom. He and I often argued within earshot of her, but she never intervened. Worse, he had a problem with my presence that remains in the realm of incomprehensibility.

"Little slut," he said under his breath when I walked by the room where he watched television.

The first time this happened, I thought I was imagining things, because my heart belonged to Bobby, and I didn't lose my virginity until age eighteen. But my stepdad kept sputtering insults.

"Slut."

"What did you say to me?"

"Nothing."

"You called me a slut."

"No I didn't."

"I *heard* you…why would you say that?"

"Go fuck yourself."

His hatred felt soul-destroying. It wasn't so much his words, but his anger behind them. I went to my mom and hoped for a safe place to land.

"Did you hear what he said?"

She didn't respond.

"Did you hear what your husband said to me?"

"I heard."

"Aren't you gonna do anything?"

"That's between the two of you."

I realized I had no protector, and decided to leave home for my own survival. It was time anyway, as I was eighteen, making me a legal adult. I rented a room in an apartment with another girl a few years older than me, working part-time at The Broadway department store to make rent. I applied to California State University Northridge, the same college Bobby attended. But after one semester, Bobby and I grew distant and broke up. I started ditching classes more frequently, because I never liked school much anyway, and college seemed like a bigger version of what I didn't like. But I knew I needed to do *something*, anything, to keep moving forward. I signed up for extension classes in broadcast journalism at UCLA, which kept me busy for a short time until a friend suggested I take classes at Los Angeles Pierce College, where, to my surprise, I found my calling. To earn my Associate Degree, I needed to take elective courses to meet basic requirements. This exploration of choices led me to journalism classes, which sparked my interest, and I attended a seminar on campus where the editor-in-chief of the student-run newspaper, the Pierce College *Roundup*, spoke. He was a tall, white, lanky teen, a chain-smoker with a deep voice. I was hooked when he spoke about the power of the press:

"Journalists have the greatest power. The press can bring justice. The press can even save lives. When people are *really* in trouble, they don't call the cops. They don't call lawyers. They call the press."

The power aspect of journalism was a big draw for me. But closing the deal: journalism would give me a voice. If I became a reporter, I could stand up for the underdogs in the pursuit of justice and righteousness. I'd have power through the written word. For so many years, I had had no power and no voice. Journalism would give me both.

Me laying out pages on a light board when I was Editor-In-Chief at the Pierce College Roundup, a student-run newspaper in Woodland Hills, California.

I joined the newspaper staff, starting as a campus reporter, and it was one of the most thrilling times in my life. By the third semester, I was editor-in-chief, and under my leadership, the newspaper earned first place in General Excellence at the 1991 Journalism Association of Community Colleges California State Competition. For the first time in my life, I felt ambitious, enthusiastic and confident. And I realized I had skills. I was a great reporter, a great writer, and above all, I had power.

At this point in my life, I reconnected with my dad and stepmom, Patty, through letters and long phone conversations. I bragged about my success as a journalist, mailing them clippings of my published articles with my byline. They acted as though no time had passed between us, were thrilled to know I found writing as my passion, and put me in touch with Jane Gilman, the editor and publisher of *The Larchmont Chronicle*, a monthly community newspaper in Los Angeles. As a nurse, my stepmom had previously connected with Jane many years prior when Patty was Jane's mother-in-law's caretaker. When Jane called me in for the interview, I respected her instantly. She was in her thirties, and one of two women running the only newspaper in small, charming Larchmont Village. This was an affluent neighborhood in central Los Angeles, notable for its quaint, charming old-town shopping street and well-maintained historic homes. Jane launched the publication with Dawne Goodwin long before the internet made it easy to lay out pages with the click of a mouse. They laid out the pages by hand in Dawne's home, and used the light from Dawne's oven to make sure the copy and photographs lined up perfectly. This operation continued until the two women made enough revenue to open an office on Larchmont Boulevard inside a converted 1920s house.

Jane and Dawne started their publication in the 1960s, a time when women didn't own and operate newspapers, which needed ad revenue to operate. They knew they wouldn't generate money from advertisers if men with deep pockets in town knew the paper was owned by women. The foresight of these two savvy businesswomen led to a smart decision. In their masthead, which appeared on page two with names of the people in charge, they used only their initials: J. Gilman and D. Goodwin. They led a staff of women and one man, who sold the ads, making the *Larchmont Chronicle* the only publication of its kind in the area. The paper solely featured community news in a place where everyone knew everyone on some level, and was quite a success.

I landed the job interview immediately because Jane loved my stepmom for the care she showed Jane's family. The first time I met Jane, she exuded lady-like confidence in a navy blue skirt with matching blazer, short manicured pink nails, her short blond hair styled to perfection. I thought to myself, *She looks like a President's wife.*

"How's Patty? How's your dad?" she asked before she spoke about the job position.

"They're great. Still living in Colorado. They have their own radio show in town. And they run a nonprofit, the Great Plains Foundation, to raise money for the needy."

"They've always cared about the community. That's one of many things I love about them. And they love you. They speak so highly of you. They tell me you're a great writer. That you love journalism."

"I do. Writing is my passion."

"Well, this job is about community journalism. You'll be on staff as a reporter. You'll re-write press releases and do some copyediting. You'll go out on assignment, interviewing local folks in town. And if there's anything you don't know how to do, I'll teach you."

"Does that mean I got the job?"

"Yes. We'd love to have you on staff."

Under Jane's guidance, I had many articles published with my byline in the *Larchmont Chronicle*, which I used to apply to the biggest metropolitan newspapers in California, including the *Los Angeles Times*. I didn't have my college degree yet, but I had grit and more confidence than ever, and knew landing a job at the *L.A. Times* would propel me up the ladder. While I was still working at the *Larchmont Chronicle*, once a month, for two years straight, I mailed the *L.A. Times* my resume and article clips. One day, I got a call from Ann, an editor at the *Times*, asking me in for an interview. I couldn't believe it. Here I was, only twenty-three years old, without a college degree, with little experience, invited to talk with the bigwigs at the biggest player in the city for the job of my dreams.

10

THE PEN IS MIGHTIER THAN THE SWORD

"If my mind can conceive it, if my heart can believe it—then I can achieve it."—Muhammad Ali

Though the main headquarters of the *L.A. Times* was in downtown Los Angeles, their building in Chatsworth, California, was a massive two-story structure with a winding staircase inside that led into the main newsroom, with a separate facility in the back for a printing press that churned nonstop to put out tens of thousands of copies each day. I entered the parking lot through a guarded gate, walked into the reception area to sign in, and waited for Ann. I didn't know what to expect of this woman, a power player as one of the main female editors in the male-dominated newsroom. I envisioned her wearing a pantsuit, perhaps even masculine in stature, exuding a look of power to match her male counterparts. When she walked down the staircase, her appearance surprised me. She was a petite woman much shorter than me, with long brown hair down to her waist, wearing a dress and heels, with a pretty, feminine face dabbed lightly with blush on her cheeks and red gloss on her lips.

"I've been wanting to meet you for some time now," Ann said to me after introducing herself. "You're the one who's been sending us your stuff once a month for two years straight. You must really want to work here."

"I just want to *be* here. I want to be a part of this."

"Have you ever seen a real newsroom before?"

"Not until now."

"How old are you?"

"Twenty-three."

"Do you have a journalism degree?"

My heart started racing. I paused before I answered, worried my lack of a college degree would break the deal. But I couldn't lie. Such facts could be verified.

"No, I don't have a degree. But I took journalism courses at Pierce College. And I was editor-in-chief of the student paper. We won awards under my leadership."

"Well, we're not hiring full-time staffers right now. But we have stringer positions. Do you know what a stringer is?"

"No."

"A stringer is a reporter who picks up the slack. They write all the stories the staffers don't want to write. They work evenings, weekends. They earn seventy-five dollars a day. And they get a byline in *The Times*."

She had me at *byline*.

"Sounds great!"

Ann smiled at my genuine enthusiasm for the job that was basically considered grunt work to the staffers.

"Well, let me show you around the newsroom and introduce you. Then we'll talk some more."

I couldn't believe I was there, finally landing the interview I worked so hard to book. When Ann escorted me into the newsroom, the energy was tangible. Phones rang nonstop, overlapped with reporters' voices, editors immersed in passionate discussions about the top stories of the day, the latest scandals, the best photos to run, deadlines to meet.

I was in awe, and thought to myself: *This is what I want. I'm meant to be here. I've waited so long for this moment.*

Ann introduced me to a few reporters, most of whom were too busy to care about my presence, some seemingly annoyed they had to break their concentration to shake my hand. But I didn't care.

"You should know you won't have your own desk," Ann told me. "Whenever you're on shift, you'll have to find an empty desk. These reporters are very protective of their space. Make sure you leave it as you found it. They can't know you were ever there."

I nodded in acknowledgment.

"You should also know some reporters here are assholes. You can't take it personally. You're a stringer, the bottom rung. They're staffers. They have huge egos. And rightfully so. They're the best of the best."

"Fine with me."

"You have a good attitude. You'll need that if you want to survive here."

After we toured the newsroom, Ann took me inside an office to sit down with two male editors. She passed my clips to them, which they flipped through without reading.

"You know what this position is about, right?" one of the men asked me.

"Yes. Ann explained it. Sounds fun. Can't wait."

"Alicia is very enthusiastic," Ann told them. "She's perfect for this."

The men exited the room before Ann brought our meeting to an end.

"Do you have any questions for me?"

"Yes. I'm wondering why it took you so long to bring me in for an interview."

"Frankly, I wanted to know who this woman was who was sending her résumé and clips for two years."

My tenacity worked. I got my foot in the door. From there, I figured everything out on the fly. And I was under the best guidance I could ask for. Ann became a female role model who helped further my career in journalism.

"Your goal here is to get your clips, get your byline in the *L.A. Times*, and get out of here as soon as possible."

Get out? I just got here. But Ann saw a bigger picture. For the next few months, I was assigned all the stories that other reporters were too busy to take on, working hours on the skeleton shift. The best part about these shifts was that nobody else was around to take on big stories when they broke. These turned into cherry assignments that appeared on the front page, sometimes above the fold, the next day with my byline. Within a few weeks, Ann told me about a job opening at the *San Diego Union Tribune*, a three-month contract position to fill in for a journalist going on maternity leave. At the time, I was living on my own in an apartment in Northridge, and made barely enough money to pay rent. Also, I was afraid of moving for a job that lasted only three months in a town where I knew nobody.

"I can't afford to move," I told Ann. "It's impossible."

"Find a way. This is a once-in-a-lifetime opportunity. Borrow the money. Put it on your credit card. Do what you have to do. This chance won't happen again."

Terrified of the unknown, I followed my instincts, fueled by Ann's faith in me. I ended my lease in Northridge, and scrounged up enough money to move to Pacific Beach in San Diego, a few miles away from the *San Diego Union Tribune*. As one of the youngest reporters there, I took on assignments relating to

Generation X, such as body-piercing trends, and covered spring break in Mexico, where underage drinking by young Americans made headline news. The three-month gig turned into six months of my byline appearing on the front page several times, which I used to land my next gig: a job at the *Los Angeles Daily News* in their satellite office in Simi Valley, where I was assigned as a community reporter, knocking out fourteen stories each week in the mid-1990s. This was an exciting time for journalists, with me competing against reporters from other publications, as well as television journalists who showed up for big stories in town. One day, out of the blue, the editor of the *Ventura County Star*, a competitor of the *Los Angeles Daily News*, contacted me. We met for lunch, where he told me he wanted to hire me as a correspondent in Simi Valley, which meant I'd have the same beat, only for a different publication. The *Ventura County Star* was smaller in circulation compared to the *Daily News*, but the salary was better, with a lighter workload of five required stories per week. I accepted this new job, and covered Simi Valley through the rest of the 1990s. In this small town of around 200,000 people, crime and education were my main beats, with a focus on special education, and I felt like a big shot working for one of the major newspapers in town.

Looking back, I believe landing a job at *The Star* was no coincidence. Fate brought me to this place. This place led me to my assignment with Robert Ortiz and Kid Gloves. And this assignment, which I pursued with reluctance at first, led to my love for boxing. With any great love, there are ups and downs, euphoria and devastating heartbreak. My love for boxing hit all sides of this emotional spectrum, and in the end, I learned the power of dedication and sacrifice, and the personal rewards that come with faith. The boxing ring is a metaphor for life, a place where the fight starts inward, and once that fight is won in the mind, anything is possible. This reminds me of a powerful quote by one of the greatest fighters of all time, a man with great insight, Muhammad Ali:

> "Champions aren't made in gyms. Champions are made from something they have deep inside them—a desire, a dream, a vision. They have to have the skill and the will. But the will must be stronger than the skill."

11 GETTING BACK IN THE GAME

"Don't quit. Suffer now and live the rest of your life as a champion."—Muhammad Ali

When I backed out of my second fight, I continued to train with Deon. In the wake of my loss, my heart wasn't in the game, but the training quieted the demons in my mind, and Deon's words of wisdom lifted my spirits and gave me clarity to move forward.

"My first loss was hard," I told him. "How do you keep going after you've lost a fight?"

"Losing is a part of life. It's what we do with our loss that matters."

"I don't know why it's so hard for me to overcome losing in the ring. I take it so personally. Like it's a sign I'm not where I'm supposed to be."

"It *is* a sign. But you're lookin' at it all wrong. You gotta adjust. Make changes. Retrain your body. Retrain your mind. When I'm stuck, I think about what James said in the bible: 'Consider it pure joy…when you face trials of many kinds, because you know that the testing of your faith produces perseverance.'"

Deon's words were inspiring, but not enough for me to get back in the ring—not yet. I still had a lot of thinking to do. And over the next few weeks, I slipped back into old bad habits, which Deon noticed every time we met to train.

"Girl, what have you been eating?"

"Everything I want."

"I can see it in your legs. You're flabby. You're slow. You can't even run a mile without heaving. Have you been smoking?"

I didn't respond, which meant yes.

"Look, you're goin' downhill, fast. You gotta get a grip on yourself. Take control. Take your power back. It's *one* loss. It shouldn't mean everything. Don't let it break you."

I started to cry.

"I don't know what to do."

"You *do* know. Now do it. I feel like quittin' all the time. But I never quit. That's one thing I never do—quit. I know what it's like to sacrifice everything. I know frustration. I know disappointment. I know the discipline it takes to be the greatest. And it's not easy. But achieving the greatest things in life is *not* easy."

"I don't know, Deon. I just don't know. I'm so confused."

"It's okay to be confused. But don't waste time in the dark. You gotta come back to the light."

Our training sessions ceased, and I didn't follow Deon's advice. I failed to own all I had accomplished at that point in boxing. I ruminated over my loss, causing a downward spiral of negativity, bringing my dark past back to the surface. The demons in my mind came back in full force. I thought I rid myself of them long ago, but here they were again. I didn't realize boxing was *the* catalyst to keep me moving forward. I was stuck in a place of self-imposed pity. The depression I grew up with bubbled to the surface, and came to a boiling point, until the pain forced me to see the truth: I didn't believe in myself, I possessed no self-love.

This had nothing to do with anyone but me. I was my own worst enemy. I finally woke up when I stepped on the scale and saw I had gained ten pounds since fighting in the Blue & Gold. I knew nobody was to blame but me.

"You better get hold of yourself," I said out loud to myself, looking in the full-length mirror. "Get your ass back in the gym."

I needed to shake things up. I decided not to go back to my old trainers, and avoided Kid Gloves, Deon and Coach. That's when I met Randy Shields, who first started boxing at the age of twelve. Working his way through the amateurs, he won eighty-eight out of ninety-two fights—with sixty-seven by knockout—and had three losses and one draw. He later went on to win six state titles and the national and international championships in 1973. He scored victories over Sugar Ray Leonard and the 1972 Olympic silver medalist from West Germany, and knocked out Roosevelt Green, the United States backup man to 1972 Olympic gold medalist Sugar Ray Seales. Sugar Ray Leonard once said, "Fighting Randy Shields is like fighting a shadow. You think he's there but he's not." Randy turned pro in 1974 and fought during the span of the next decade. He had over sixty pro fights, scoring twenty-eight knockouts. He fought eight out of the top ten contenders as a lightweight, defeating them all.

I met Randy when I attended a boxing match in the San Fernando Valley, and he worked the corner of Robert's brother, Victor. Victor's wife Shannon and I were still at odds as two women in the same weight class trying to make our names, but I wanted to support her and her husband, and hoped to smooth things over by going to the match. Shannon and I didn't speak much to each other after my first exhibition against Layla, as I still believed they recruited her to knock me out. I never called Shannon out on the matter. I felt it would be poor sportsmanship, and I wanted to keep my reputation in the boxing world as a woman who supported other women in the ring. After Victor's fight, which he won by a spectacular knockout, I went into his dressing room to congratulate him and his wife. Randy was there, too, praising Victor for putting on a great show. Victor and Shannon were gracious with my presence, and Randy noticed me right away.

"Hi, I'm Randy Shields,"

"I know who you are." I blushed in the presence of the fighter I viewed as a big-time celebrity.

"Are you a boxer, too?"

"Yes. Amateur."

"Do you have a trainer?"

"Sort of. I train with Robert Ortiz and Stan Ward. They're great. But I wanna learn more skills. New skills."

I gave Randy the rundown on my ambitions, losing my first amateur match, and my indecisiveness about getting back in the game.

"How long has it been since you trained?"

"A few weeks. I'm pretty rusty."

Victor chimed in.

"She might be rusty but that girl can throw a left jab like nobody's business. You should see how hard she trains."

Randy looked at me from head to toe.

"What weight class are you in?"

"I fought 129 at nationals. I've gained weight. But I can drop."

"Yeah, you need to lean out. I'd love to work with you. But I'll tell ya right now, I'm not gonna take it easy on you."

"That's exactly what I need."

"Here's my card. Be at the gym on Monday."

"The day after tomorrow?"

"Is that a problem for you?"

"No sir. I'll be there."

On Monday, I almost got lost trying to find Randy's gym, a nondescript storefront tucked off the beaten path among similar one-story buildings in an industrial area of Van Nuys. His gym was private, mainly for professional boxers and big-name amateur fighters, and I was the only woman there. As I walked in, the pungent smell of men punctuated the thickness of the air, with at least a half-dozen guys dripping pools of sweat onto the concrete floor. The grimace on my face at the stench made Randy laugh.

"Not what you're used to, huh?'

I didn't want him to think I couldn't stomach the stink.

"It's all good."

For several weeks, I trained one-on-one with Randy, who kept his promise: he was harder on me than any other trainer in the past. I welcomed his insight, starting with the basics.

Punching the heavy bag, "You gotta imagine that's your opponent. Only the heavy bag doesn't hit back."

Skipping rope, "You gotta move. Use the *whole* floor. Skip around the bags. Pretend you're dancin' in the ring with your opponent."

Doing 200 sit-ups, "Don't start countin' until it hurts. When you're in pain, that's when it starts to count."

Smacking the focus mitts, "The combination's gotta flow without thought. The double-jab, right and left hook gotta come outta ya like second nature."

This execution also required visualization.

"You gotta *imagine* it before you can do it. When you're not here, spend time every day imagining yourself in a fight. See yourself slippin' your opponent's punches. See yourself connectin' with each jab. See yourself knockin' girls out."

Randy gave me few, if any, compliments. His honesty was brutal, like the time he whacked me with his left hook when I dropped my guard.

"You're shitty at keepin' your hands up."

"Fuck! I keep forgetting."

"Forgettin' will get you knocked out. Do better."

I tried again, but as soon as I grew tired, my hands dropped, and I got punched.

"You know I'm takin' it easy on you, right? You're not takin' this seriously enough. Droppin' your hands can cost you your head, your life. The next time you drop your hands, I'm gonna knock you out."

"Knock me out? We're only sparring…"

"Only sparring?!" Randy yelled across the gym for all the fighters to hear. "You think because you're a girl you can get away with takin' it easy? This is *boxing*, baby. The hurt business. You don't wanna get hurt, get the fuck outta my ring."

"I'm sorry Randy. I was out of line."

"You're damn right you were outta line. I'm teachin' you this stuff so you don't get hurt. I'm helpin' you. You're not helpin' me. You don't wanna play anymore? Then get the fuck outta here and let the big boys play."

"I'm here to play."

"Then keep your fuckin' hands up!"

Randy's demand sent a shock through my entire body. But it worked. In the next round of sparring, my gloves didn't budge from protecting both sides of my face when Randy threw his shots.

"That's what I'm talkin' about! You stopped fightin' like a girl!"

Boxing is all about conditioned responses, takes years to perfect, and even then, a boxer keeps learning. I couldn't expect to learn everything I needed to know overnight. Also, I had to accept the fact that, as with life, things don't always work out in my favor in the ring.

"You have to be ready for disappointment," Randy said one night after our worst training session. On this night, Randy socked me in the liver. The punch wasn't hard, but so precise, I fell down. I'd never been dropped before. The shot paralyzed me.

"You okay?"

"Yes," I said, buckled over.

"You get it now, right?"

"The hurt business."

"Yes. A world of hurt. You still wanna do this?"

"I wanna keep training. I wanna keep learning. But the more I learn, the less I know. Does it ever end?"

"Never. And it shouldn't. If it did, might as well be dead."

Me hitting the heavy bag at the gym of my trainer, Randy Shields.

THE WORLD OF BOXING is small. Coach heard through word of mouth that I was training with Randy, but his support remained like we never parted. At least once a week, he called to check in on my mental and physical state. Hearing his voice on the other line brought me comfort, especially after a grueling training session with Randy.

"I hear you're doin' great at Randy's. The men aren't used to seein' a tough girl over there. You doin' okay? You feelin' okay?"

"I'm good. Randy's great. But I miss you. I miss Deon. Are you mad at me for leaving?"

"No. Never. We understand why you left. You took that loss hard. I think part of you believed we were at fault. Fighters blame their corners. It happens."

"I never blamed you. I knew that loss was on me. But yes. I did take it hard. Too hard. I took it personally. I'm still trying to figure that part out. Why I take losing so personally."

"Because it's part of you. Boxing's part of your soul, your identity. So when you lost, it was like you lost your identity. But what you failed to realize is the truth."

"What truth?"

"*You* are your identity. And you'll always have you. No matter what. Nobody can take you away from you."

After a long pause, Coach told me the timely reason he called. He and his wife were celebrating their wedding anniversary, and wanted to invite me to the party at a fancy home in Bel Air owned by their friends. I was nervous about seeing Coach again. It seemed like so much time passed. But when I walked in the door, he wrapped me in his gigantic arms. So many thoughts raced through my head. With Coach in my corner, we went through battles together, but I left him cold-turkey with no word about coming back. I abandoned him, but he remained, waiting until the day I was ready. Coach knew I was on the fence about boxing, but that didn't seem to matter much to him. He got it.

"I'm so sorry, Coach."

"Sorry? For what?"

"For leaving you. For not explaining why. I left without saying anything."

"You didn't have to. We knew why. Fighters know what it's like in the ring. It's like being naked in front of the world. It's like you're fightin' the world. But really, you're fightin' yourself. And you only find yourself when you fight yourself, when you face and overcome your *self*."

"...that's deep."

"Boxing *is* deep. Deeper than most people think."

"I need to come back. I want to come back. I need to get back in the game."

Coach and I were immersed in conversation when Deon walked up. He looked magnificent. While I was away, he was earning his rank as the number four amateur boxer in the nation. To my surprise, another special guest was there, Lucia Rijker, also known as "Lady Tyson," with a boxing record of seventeen wins and zero losses, with fourteen wins by knockout.

She was the real deal, a ferocious, beautiful fighter best known for her role in the boxing film *Million Dollar Baby* alongside Hilary Swank and Clint Eastwood. Lucia played the fighter who punched Hilary Swank's character into a vegetative state.

Now the question was, what do I do next? Stay with Randy? Go back to Coach? Return to Kid Gloves? I decided to go back where it all began, Kid Gloves, and started training solo to clear my head. Robert welcomed me, no questions asked.

"You have to get back where you used to be," he said upon my return. "Have confidence in yourself. Remember who you are."

Shortly after I went back to Robert's gym, I reconnected with a man I wrote an article about, Jim Mullen, who also trained at Kid Gloves. Jim was a champion of Draka, a Russian school of kickboxing with takedowns. Oddly, in contrast with the intense violence in his sport, Jim was deeply religious, and used his platform as a fighter to spread the word of Jesus Christ. Six feet five inches tall and 220 pounds, Jim won many Draka fights, and attributed his wins to God. He always talked about the Lord, and wore bible scripture numbers on his boxer shorts in the ring. When Jim saw me at Kid Gloves, he took a break from training to greet me.

"Good to see you back. Are you here to stay?"

"I hope so…"

"I heard you lost your first fight."

"Yeah. It was hard. I thought about quitting. But the longer I stayed away, the worse I felt."

"When you return from a loss stronger, that's the mark of a true champion."

I also reconnected with Bridgett "Baby Doll" Riley, who occasionally trained at Kid Gloves. She held the IFBA's world Bantamweight championship for a short period of time, and was managed by Don King for several years. I knew about Bridgett because she was one of the few women in America at the time getting paid for boxing at a competitive level. She was one of the pioneers who cleared the way for women like me to enter the male-dominated sport. When I saw her at Kid Gloves, I expressed my thoughts about quitting.

"*Don't* quit," Bridgett told me. "If I would've quit, I wouldn't be a champion."

I decided to keep going, and continued to train with the same intensity as when I prepared for the National Blue & Gold. I was in the midst of one of my workouts when Robert made me take a break, because he had some news.

"The 1999 Golden Gloves is coming up. I want you to fight for the title."

The National Golden Gloves contest began in 1962, and continues to be the most highly regarded amateur boxing tournament in the United States. Many amateur Golden Gloves participants went on to become professional boxers, including Joe Louis, Muhammad Ali and Joe Frazier. I was getting back in tip-top shape, so I agreed, but still had doubts.

"Me? A Golden Gloves Champ?"

Robert didn't like to hear my confidence wane, and he repeated a lesson he gives his child boxers after their training sessions.

"Remember what I tell the kids, the ABCs backwards: Conceive, Believe, Achieve. You can do this!"

The thought of winning a Golden Gloves Championship was too thrilling to pass up, which meant dropping weight, training like a maniac, and the most important factor—keeping my mind strong for the fight. All of a sudden, I was back in the game, with Robert in my corner. His son, Bobby, became my regular sparring partner, and Robert's brother, Danny, came on board as one of my trainers. The more days that passed with them, the more confident I became.

I was feeling on top of the world, when Robert told me another woman from Kid Gloves also entered the Golden Gloves: Shannon.

"I'm fighting your sister-in-law for the title?"

"Probably. She's in your weight class."

"Won't that be weird for you? Her husband, *your* brother, will be working her corner."

"It's not the first time this has happened, brothers working opposite corners. Besides, we're not the ones getting in the ring."

For the next several weeks, Shannon and I trained at Kid Gloves, both knowing we'd face off on fight night. At times, it was hard for me to concentrate on training, especially when Shannon whispered nasty comments about me behind my back. This was unnerving—we were vying for the same title, why couldn't we show mutual respect and sportsmanship? We were both breaking ground in a male-dominated sport, giving us both a platform to be positive role models for women. These thoughts distracted me as I hit the focus gloves with Robert, and Shannon and her trainer stared at me from across the room. I kept missing the mitts, and Robert knew my mind was elsewhere.

"You better wake up, Alicia Doyle."

12
VICTORY

"You can't go into the ring and be a nice guy."
—Jake LaMotta

With the Golden Gloves tournament slated a few days after Easter Sunday in 1999, I prepared for the pinnacle of the amateur boxing experience. I signed up about six weeks before the competition, giving me plenty of time to train at Kid Gloves. These preparation days were grueling. I woke up at four a.m. to run before sunrise, and arrived in the newsroom at eight a.m. sharp. The moment my shift ended at five p.m., I went to the bathroom to change from my work clothes into my boxing gear. Like mild-mannered reporter Clark Kent turning into Superman in a phone booth, I'd emerge in my tattered sweatpants, oversized T-shirt and hand wraps.

To my surprise, the fear of getting knocked out or losing went by the wayside. I had survived a standing eight and losing my first fight, and going through those experiences strengthened my resolve and made me feel like I could survive anything that came my way.

The 1999 Golden Gloves took place in Lincoln Park in East Los Angeles, where the gym was packed for one of the biggest boxing competitions of the year. While the number of girls in the sport was growing, we were still few compared to the men who showed up to compete. I weighed in at 137 pounds, and the commissioners confirmed Shannon would be my opponent. The crowd included Latino parents who came to see their sons in the ring.

"La guarda! La guarda!" one father shouted through his son's match to remind the boy to keep his guard up.

Also in attendance were the local kids, blue-clad, heavily tattooed African-American teens. But they were on their best behavior, just there to enjoy the fights. Of course, many people from Kid Gloves got word that Shannon and I were fighting, and showed up to root us on. Even though we were going to be enemies in that square, we both received the same loving support from the people at Kid Gloves who had watched us train in the gym for weeks. Before the fight, I naturally had a bit of fear, mostly because I believed Shannon hated me and wanted to take me out with every ounce of her being. As soon as our match was announced, Shannon's friends and my friends clamored to get seats close to the ring. I saw both groups out of the corner of my eye, and tried to ignore the insults from the friends of my competitor. I wanted to strike back with words, but developed a level of sportsmanship I felt was important to convey as a female boxer, and kept my mouth shut.

Shannon and I climbed into the ring, went to our corners, and I saw a look of sheer hatred in her eyes. Robert remained calm as he knelt down to give me a boost of wisdom before the starting bell.

"Do your best. That's all you need to do."

In the first round, Shannon came out swinging, charging at me like a raging bull. I slipped her punches, and saved my energy, because I knew her misses sucked the life out of her. She grew weary quickly, and I took my shots, nailing her with precision each time I shot a jab and hard right. The more jabs I threw, the more Shannon backed up, and the crowd went nuts, fueling my adrenaline through the roof. After the first round, we went back to our corners, and Robert wiped the sweat off my shoulders, gave me a drink of water and told me how to proceed.

"Keep doing what you're doing. It's working. How do you feel?"

"Fucking *great*!"

"Good," Robert said with a laugh. "But the fight's not over yet…"

I didn't give him eye contact. I focused on Shannon in her corner, watched her heave and wondered how long she'd last. When we faced off again in round two, one word went through my mind: *annihilate.* I threw my straight right at her face and followed with body blows, smack after smack after smack. I kept on punching when she cowered and covered herself with both arms. When she dropped her guard, I went after her harder. The rest bell hadn't rung yet when the referee stepped in between us, and faced me with both arms outward.

"Go back to your corner!"

I didn't listen, and tried to move around him. My animal instincts told me to eliminate the threat, no matter what. That threat was Shannon.

"Go *back* to your corner!" the ref demanded again. "*Stop!* I said *stop!*"

I ignored him and moved toward Shannon, with my right fist cocked ready to blow. She clearly couldn't go on, and bent over lifeless in the middle of the ring.

"Stop!" Robert yelled from my corner. "You'll get penalized!"

When I finally obeyed, the ref shot me a look like he wanted to strangle me. I didn't follow his orders, which were paramount in this game, and in that moment, I didn't care. The emotions I felt were delightful in the sickest way—I enjoyed beating the shit out of Shannon, who had dissed me for so long. I rode the wave of this twisted elation for a few seconds, when I realized the fight was over. I looked Shannon's way, and to my surprise, felt horrible for what I saw: she slumped red-faced, exhausted and visibly hurt, as her husband put his arms around her.

I snapped back into the moment when I heard the crowd cheering my name. I won by technical knockout when the referee stopped the contest. That night, I became the 1999 Golden Gloves Champion.

"I can't believe it," I told Robert after the win.

"Believe it! I knew you could do it! We *all* knew you could do it!"

Walking down from the ring, I was engulfed by fans, who asked for my autograph and stood at my side to take pictures.

Robert seemed the most proud. "This is something nobody can ever take away from you. This will always be a part of you."

The referee raising my hand in victory after I won the 1999 Golden Gloves Championship in Los Angeles.

13

PARADIGM SHIFT

"Champions aren't made in gyms. Champions are made from something they have deep inside them—a desire, a dream, a vision. They have to have the skill, and the will. But the will must be stronger than the skill."—Muhammad Ali

After my victory against Shannon, my trainers started planning my next amateur match—another Golden Gloves Championship in a place that seemed like the middle of nowhere. The match was on July 31, 1999, in Tulare, California, named after the dried up Tulare Lake located in the heart of the Central Valley. With three months to prepare for the fight, I knew I'd be ready. Shannon avoided Kid Gloves for weeks after our match, and I wondered if she was okay, if she still hated me, if she was still talking smack. I was in the gym alone training, hitting the heavy bag, when I saw a woman with long wavy red hair walk in, wearing a dress like she was going to church. It was Shannon.

"Can I talk to you?" she asked with a tone of kindness I had never heard her speak before.

"Sure," I said as I took off my gloves. "What's up?"

"I want to apologize to you."

I didn't know what to say, and didn't respond.

"I know how I treated you all this time. I was a bitch. And I'm really sorry. You didn't deserve it."

I couldn't believe the words coming out of her mouth.

"It's okay, Shannon..."

"No. It's not okay. I should have been more supportive. I'm here to apologize...ask your forgiveness."

In that moment, my heart softened for the woman I had beaten up just weeks before.

"Of course I forgive you."

"Thank you," she said, and embraced me.

"I hardly recognized you when you walked in. You look so pretty dressed up."

"Yeah, I clean up well," she said with a laugh. "So, I hear you're fighting again. In Tulare. Another Golden Gloves."

"Yeah. I really don't know what to expect."

"Do you know anything about your opponent?"

"Not really. Just that she's the home-town girl."

"Well, I know you're gonna do great. You're a great fighter."

On the day of the match in Tulare, Robert was there to work my corner, along with my friend Debbie, a super lightweight amateur boxer I met at Kid Gloves. The three of us left early in the morning for weigh-ins, and it took us nearly three hours to drive to the fight venue, where I discovered my opponent, Lisa, was a teenager who worked as a waitress in town. I was an outsider coming into her territory, and she arrived with a crowd of fans, overshadowing my two-person support system.

After the weigh-ins, several bouts with the boys took place before ours. I sat in the corner of a quiet room on-site to think and stretch, like I always did before a fight, when three girls from Lisa's posse came by to size me up. They walked past me, again and again, gave me dirty looks, and said a few things in Spanish.

"Puta anciana."

"Ella es muy vieja."

"Lisa la va a matar!"

I was visibly much older than Lisa, so they likely believed she could easily take an old lady out. But I ignored their glares, blew off their words, and stayed focused on the fight.

"What'd they say to you?" Robert asked when he came by to check on me.

"I dunno. I don't speak Spanish. But I *think* they called me an old lady or something."

Robert laughed.

"I guess you *are* compared to Lisa. She's just a kid."

"Yeah. Well, that *kid* is the star of the show today. Seems like everyone's here to see her fight."

"They are. She's the home-town girl. That means the fight's already in her favor. You can't just outpoint her. You're gonna have to knock her out if you wanna win."

"What do you mean I can't just outpoint her? There's a ref. There are judges."

"That doesn't mean anything. She's *their* hometown girl. If the fight is close, they'll give *her* the win."

"That's fucked."

"That's boxing."

I'd heard about boxers getting "robbed" but I never thought it would happen to me, especially in amateurs. I wanted to believe the sport was pure, but the truth of the matter was, corruption existed on all levels in boxing.

Robert saw by the look on my face that I didn't like the reason behind his strategy.

"I can tell you're mad…use that anger in the ring. Come out strong like you always do. Don't back down no matter what. Work that jab, all day long. And if you see an opening, knock her out."

A tiny crowd filled the room during the boys' fights until Lisa and I stepped in the ring. When our names were called and we went to our corners, it was standing room only, with her fans packing the room.

"Remember what I told you," Robert instructed before the starting bell.

Lisa came out in a flurry, just like Shannon did in my fight at the Golden Gloves. I slipped and weaved through Lisa's punches and threw few of my own, assuming she'd tire out early. I saw her hands drop, threw my jab, and broke her nose within thirty seconds. It was the first time I broke a woman's nose in competition, and I never saw so much blood in my life gush from a person's face. My jab scored each time, so I used it again, and again, and again. But Lisa remained strong. She kept fighting, connecting with a few counterpunches to my body when my gloves were up protecting my face.

Damn, I thought to myself. *This kid is tough.*

"Jab!" Robert screamed. "Jab! Jab! Jab!"

"Golpearla en el cuerpo!" her cornerman yelled. "Los golpes al cuerpo están funcionando!"

Every time I threw my jab, I connected with her nose, making her bleed harder each time. A stream of red poured down her lips and chin, spilled down the front of her tank top, and spattered on the ring mat.

I looked at the ref for a moment to gage his reaction, and wondered if he'd stop the fight. But this was her backyard, I was in her house, and there was no way in hell our referee was going to make this Tulare girl the loser. After round one, I went back to my corner, where Robert surprised me with his assessment.

"The fight's too close. She got in some good shots. You gotta work harder."

"She's bleeding all over the fuckin' place. She's hurt. The ref needs to stop the fight."

"He's *not* gonna stop the fight."

"Fuck!"

"The jab is workin'…two rounds to go. If you see an opening, *knock her out*."

Lisa looked exhausted in her corner as her coach wiped the blood from her face. But when the bell rang for round two, she came out again in full force, even though she couldn't breathe through her nose anymore. I saw she was in pain, and I wanted to ease up, but I wanted to win even more. My jab worked every time to score points, so I hit her again, and again, and again. She couldn't figure out how to block my jab, so her nose was my main target, forcing a sea of red with each blow. At the end of round two, I was so exhausted, I was happy the fight was almost over with only one more round left to go.

"This fight is *hard*," I told Robert in my corner. "She's *tough*. She's wearin' me out."

"You won that round for sure. But she *still* might win if it goes to the scorecards."

"I'm sick of the blood. I just wanna get outta here."

"One more round. You can do this. Give it everything you got."

Lisa's corner must have told her the same thing, because she came out in round three like she was fighting for her life. When I punched her in her broken nose, she counterpunched with a body shot. When I hit her in the body, she threw a straight right to my face. Her punches were weak in round three compared to round one, but they still hurt, and I couldn't help but respect this girl for taking so much punishment and continuing to fight. And what was it all for? Bragging rights? A plastic trophy? What if I did permanent damage to her nose?

What if she needed plastic surgery? Would I be able to live with myself?

Finally, the fight was over, and I was relieved. But I also worried over what Robert told me. What if she got the win? It was obvious I outpointed her. But what if the corruption he spoke of took that win away from me? I trained hard for this fight, starved for weeks to make weight, sacrificed time with friends and family to prepare.

"If she gets the win, I'm gonna be pissed," I told Robert as the judges tallied up the scores.

"You *won* this fight."

"But what if they give it to her?"

"We'll suck it up."

"That is so *wrong*."

The referee motioned Lisa and me into the center of the ring. The crowd roared on its feet, chanting her name. Standing between us, the ref raised my hand as the winner. The audience booed at my victory, and even though I didn't know much Spanish, I knew what "*Mierda!*" meant. Robert and Debbie embraced me and gave me high fives as the rest of the audience surrounded Lisa. I made my way through this thick crowd to speak to her face-to-face. I felt I owed it to this girl to congratulate her for stepping in the ring, to thank her for giving me the opportunity to fight. As I worked my way through her fans, they looked at me with confusion when I embraced her.

"That was a *hard* fight," I told her. "You're a *tough* girl."

"*You're* tough!"

"You know you're remarkable, right?"

"What do you mean?"

"You stepped in that square. Not many women have the guts to box."

"I never thought of that."

"It's true. And you got hurt. You kept going. I know I hurt you, but you kept going. You never gave up."

"Yeah. You busted my nose."

"I'm sorry. Are you okay?"

"Yeah. I'll be okay."

Our exchange in front of her fans seemed to soften them a bit, as their glares turned to the slightest smiles. It was a pinnacle moment of sportsmanship I was able to pay forward, thanks to what Layla taught me months before. But something else happened I didn't expect: I felt bad for hurting Lisa. Even though I won, I didn't feel good about it. I was being rewarded for an act of violence. I won my second championship—another Golden Gloves title—by hurting a teenage girl. These thoughts brought me back to the violence I witnessed as a child. Every time my parents fought, the energy in our home became toxic. With each screaming match they had, a suffocating, invisible, dark energy remained. It was the same energy of darkness I felt after beating Lisa. Because of this, instead of feeling elated, I felt emotionally depleted after our match. When I got home, I begged God for forgiveness. I got down on my knees and cried.

"What's wrong with me? What am I trying to prove?"

14 FORGIVENESS

"It isn't the mountains ahead to climb that wear you out; it's the pebble in your shoe."—Muhammad Ali

After more than two decades of being without each other, my dad and I started to communicate more often by phone. I welcomed our talks and the chance to re-establish our relationship through boxing, which served as a catalyst for our new connection. My dad had boxed in the Navy, and when I told him I followed in his footsteps—that I was a trailblazer in a sport dominated by men—he was proud. We both shared the experience of battle in the ring, and bonded over the physical and emotional tolls only a boxer could understand.

"I'm not surprised, baby girl. You always were a fighter."

"What do you mean, Dad?"

"You got knocked down a lot. You got hurt a lot. But you always bounced back. You're a fighter…you fight. When things get hard, you fight."

"I never saw it that way."

"How could you? When we're in the fight, we don't see it. We're too busy fighting. It's literal. It's internal. It's all-encompassing. It's hard at times. But it's a beautiful thing."

"Beautiful?"

"The human condition is a beautiful thing."

"What does the human condition have to do with fighting?"

"The human condition *is* fighting. It's part of what we're here to do. It's part of what we're here to learn."

"That's pretty deep, Dad."

"Yes. It is. You don't see the depth because you're in it. You're immersed in it. And boxing is a part of your depth, your fight… part of your journey."

"I know boxing changed me…it *is* changing me. But I don't know to what end. I love it. And I hate it. Boxing is the hardest thing I've ever done in my life. I want to quit. But I can't stay away."

"That's why you have to keep going."

"I'm not ready to quit…yet."

"You'll figure it out. Trust yourself, baby girl. And remember, I'm always here for you. And you have Tony, too."

"Tony?"

"Your brother."

"I know who he is. I just haven't reached out to him."

"He's your *brother*. You should reach out. He'd love to see you. He'd love to hear about your life, your boxing. You know you're his only sister, right? He lost his other sister. We lost her years ago…"

"Monica…"

"Yes, Monica."

"I'm sorry. I know it's painful talking about Monica."

"It's okay baby… Life is painful sometimes. But we gotta keep fighting, right?"

Hearing my dad's voice solidified my desire to meet Tony, a son from my dad's first marriage. For many years prior, my dad and stepmother tried to reunite Tony and me, but for whatever reason, I wasn't ready—or willing—to make the connection. Perhaps our similarities were too painful to address, and part of me worried that Tony was indirectly angry with me. We both grew up without our father, with Tony's void caused when our dad left his first family to be with my mom.

I never had a clear plan in mind to meet Tony, but one day, after training, I decided it was time. He worked at the Toyota car dealership in the San Fernando Valley, less than five miles away from my apartment in Sherman Oaks. For years, I had driven by the dealership, knowing Tony might be working, but I never mustered up the courage to stop by and introduce myself. On the day I decided to meet him face-to-face, I was filled with an emptiness I couldn't understand. Everything was going great in my life, or so it seemed. I was earning a stellar reputation as a female breaking the glass ceiling in the world of boxing. I was well-respected in the journalism world. I was in the best shape of my life. But my heart still ached with an incomprehensible void. As I drove by the car dealership, something prompted me pull into the parking lot, an invisible force of sorts, something bigger than myself. I walked into the showroom and approached a salesman.

"Can I help you?"

"Yes. I'm here to see Tony Doyle."

"He's here. What's your name?"

"Alicia Doyle."

The salesman looked puzzled when I said my name, as though perhaps I was Tony's ex-wife, and in no way a blood relative, because Tony is white and I'm Asian-American, making us too different to be familial.

"Does he know you're here?"

"No."

The salesman escorted me to Tony's office, where I waited about thirty minutes before a man walked in. He looked just like my dad, only decades younger. I noticed his hands, which looked like my dad's, with fair skin speckled slightly with freckles. The striking resemblance left me speechless, until Tony reached out his hand to shake mine.

"Who are you?"

"Alicia Doyle."

Tony paused in silence before speaking again.

"I know who you are."

He asked me to wait and walked out of his office, where I sat for more than an hour. I wondered where he went, why he was gone for so long, if he called a friend in shock that his sister came to his office, the sister he never met. When he returned, Tony nonchalantly asked if I wanted to get sushi, and I was surprised he liked one of my favorite foods. When Tony spoke, his voice reminded me of my dad, bringing me back to the days my dad's presence filled my heart with joy. We drove separate cars to the sushi place on Ventura Boulevard in the San Fernando Valley, where Tony sat us at the sushi bar instead of a table, loosened and removed his tie after his long day at work, and undid the first two buttons on his white, long-sleeved shirt. His movements seemed to occur in slow motion, once again reminding me of my dad. We ordered sake and fancy sushi rolls, and as we drank and ate for two hours, I was surprised at my brother's chopstick skills, which my mother taught me how to master when I was four. We instantly clicked, like no time had passed, like we were always close, like we were best friends as brother and sister our entire lives. My brother's dry sense of humor surprised me, and how much he made me laugh with his wry wit, much like our dad. I expected anger and resentment from Tony toward me, considering who I was and what I represented: the daughter of the mistress who broke up his family. But there was no dissension between us. We became inseparable, and started making up for lost time. I learned Tony was divorced from his first wife, whom he met in high school. They wed as soon as they discovered they were pregnant with their first child, Desiree, and after having their second child, Trenton, the marriage fell apart. Tony remained in his children's lives as best he could, and often referred to the mother of his children as "a saint."

My brother lived with deep regret and guilt, more than he could endure at times, knowing he repeated the pattern of our dad. Tony immersed me in his life, and the lives of his children, whom I saw on Wednesday nights and every other weekend when he had custody. These were some of the happiest times in my life, as the precious innocence of Trenton and Desiree was a light in my inner world of darkness. On the days and nights I spent with my brother, niece and nephew, salmon was our typical dinner of choice, with salads made from fresh lettuce and tomatoes picked from Tony's garden in the backyard. We spent our days playing at a local park, where my nephew's sweetness shined through on many occasions, like the time he sat in a patch filled with clovers and dandelions, looked down at the greenery, and yelled across the field.

"Auntie! Come look!"

"What'd you find?"

"A four-leaf clover," he exclaimed, grasping the weed gently with his tiny fingers like it was the most precious find on earth.

"Wow…pretty, isn't it?"

"Yes. I wanna give it to you."

Desiree enjoyed playing with dolls, and understood societal hierarchy, which she conveyed at a young age when she pulled five Barbies and one Ken from her toy box. One by one, she designated each doll's place, setting them neatly side by side.

"This is the rich girl. This is the poor girl. This is the smart girl. This is the dumb girl. This is the mean girl."

"What about Ken?" I asked her.

She grabbed the Ken doll, threw it across the room, and his plastic body smacked against the wall.

"Ken's at work."

EVEN THOUGH MY DAD and I were communicating more often, I harbored some resentment. I discussed this openly with Tony, and while he held anger, too, he stood up for our dad. I trusted Tony, so I listened.

"You gotta let that shit go," he told me. "I got a lot to be pissed about, too. But our dad could be dead tomorrow."

"I just wish he could have been there for me growing up. I'd be a different person now."

"You *are* the person you *are* because he wasn't there. Yeah, we had it hard, growing up without dad. But that made us who we are."

My brother's wisdom was poignant because his pain far outweighed mine. Years after my dad left his first family for my mom, Tony's sister, Monica, died. The two were best friends, inseparable growing up, and Tony was still in high school when Monica prepared for college. One night, she was at a party, where she drank alcohol and imbibed other substances. She was taking antidepressants at the time, and the toxic mix made her fall into a coma for a year. In the time leading up to her death, Tony often sat at her bedside in the hospital, talking to his sister, watching her waste away.

"Do you think if dad stuck around Monica would still be alive?" I asked him.

"It's irrelevant. Dad left. My sister died. It is what it is. Nothing I can do about it..."

Tony's matter-of-fact details about Monica were removed and distant, like he recited a story that belonged to someone else. His recount had to be told that way. Otherwise, the memory might have broken him.

"I try to focus on the now," he told me. "When you came back into my life, I felt like God gave me another sister…hating our dad doesn't help anything. And he had a hard life, too."

"What do you mean? He never really talks about his past."

"Well, from what I've heard, it was pretty bad."

I wanted to know more about my dad's history, so I reunited with his two older sisters, whom I hadn't spoken to since my parents' divorce. The three of us visited my dad's childhood home in Southern California, where my grandparents' house looked like a shack, a makeshift structure built of wooden planks. In the kitchen, the floor dipped in the center, caused by moisture from humidity and weight of a family of five crossing the small space every day. My aunts took me into the bedroom the three of them shared as children, where an old bunk bed and narrow cot remained.

We sat in that room for hours as my aunts revealed the horrid abuse my dad endured, physical and emotional, at the hands of my grandfather, an alcoholic with a violent side. My grandmother was an alcoholic, too, but never abused my dad the way my grandfather did. I learned my dad's childhood was full of fear and humiliation. His father berated him for being no good, for being stupid, that he'd never amount to anything more than a truck driver. After my grandfather pushed my dad down a flight of stairs in one of his drunken rages, my dad became reclusive for many years, and in the safe space of his own mind, honed his brilliance as an engineer. I never knew specific details about my dad's past until my aunts told me. And he had no reason to share this information with me. He had to fix his life and move on, the best way he could, with the tools he possessed.

This newfound wisdom filled my psyche as I began to

train for my next boxing match in Southern California, where my opponent and I were the only two women fighting on the undercard of pro boxing matches featuring male fighters. Days before the fight, my dad and I talked at length on the phone.

"Are you prepared?" he asked.

"As prepared as I'll ever be..."

"What do you know about your opponent?"

"Her name is Julie. She's strong. She's got long arms. And she's already won a few fights."

"Don't think about that too much...how good *she* is. How strong *she* is."

"Isn't that important? So I'm prepared going in?"

"Not as important as how strong *you* are. How good *you* are. Don't give too much energy to her. Focus on you. See yourself winning before you step in the ring."

"What if I lose?"

"What if you lose?"

"Will you still be proud of me?"

"Baby girl...I will always be proud of you. I've always been proud of you. The question is...are you proud of yourself? Are *you* happy?"

"I'm trying, Dad."

15

THE HURT BUSINESS

"Something's bound to happen to you in a tough fight: cut eye, broken nose or broken hand or something like that. So you could make excuses out of anything, you know, but you got to keep on going if you're a champ or you're a contender."—Jake LaMotta

My head wasn't in the game in my match against Julie. The fight went to the scorecards in the end, and I lost by a few points. But this time, I didn't care too much about winning or losing. Greater victories were in play. My big brother and his children made a place for me in their lives. My dad was back, filling the void I felt for years. I never dreamed that boxing would create a strong connection between my dad and me. The hurt between us melted away, making space for new memories, every time we talked on the phone.

"It's okay you lost that fight," he said when I gave him the news.

"It sucks, Dad. But the loss doesn't hurt like it did before."

"That's good…Sometimes, losing is a good thing."

"How?"

"Losing makes us reassess. Refocus. Restructure how we look

at things. Life isn't all about winning. Life is about loss. Loss is what makes us. Sometimes, when you lose, you win."

"I'll remember that in my next fight."

My dad's words meant everything as I prepared for my next match—the most challenging of my amateur boxing career. This elimination tournament, the 1999 National Blue & Gold at Baldwin Park in Los Angeles, involved fighting three days in a row. Days leading up to the event, my dad boosted my confidence in an email:

> You own the competitors in your division. They are yours. They can't hurt you. They are all the pain and hurt the world has bestowed upon you. Your time is now to destroy those that would take, those who would pain our girl. All your hopes and all your dreams are here, now, in the ring. This is your life to emerge the winner you have always been. Your enemies in the ring see the strength in your eyes and in your technique. They have been overcome by total fear. They're down. They all fall early in the fight. You're too fast, they're too slow. They hit you, you don't feel the pain. They're down. You're the winner.

The National Blue & Gold competition seemed exciting, yet insignificant. Exciting because my head was back in the game, insignificant compared to releasing the resentment I harbored toward my dad. He was present and accessible, like no time had passed. I realized the time I lost, distracted by self-imposed misery over what I couldn't get back. Living in the past wasn't working anymore. I looked forward, with my dad now virtually in my corner.

The 1999 National Blue & Gold was a big deal for women boxers, this time because there were more of us competing from all over the United States. It was also a big deal for me personally, because I had never boxed three days in a row, back-to-back. In my previous matches, it took me at least two weeks to fully recover from the body blows, head shots and face punches. There was no way training could condition my body to take the punishment I was about to face.

The tournament took place inside the same recreation center I fought the prior year—Baldwin Park, a community that FBI crime data determined was not the safest in America. Boxing matches in towns like this weren't unusual, as many, especially in Los Angeles, were staged in such places. But the danger didn't lie in the venue location and its surroundings. The imminent danger was inside the ring, where if a fighter won by knockout—and by small chance killed her opponent with a lethal blow to the head—she could go home victorious without fear of punishment.

Weeks before the match, I spent time with Tony, who showed no support for his little sister stepping in the ring. This was the first time a strain occurred between us since we met. Preparing for fights, I knew the importance of maintaining a positive mindset, making his input impossible to endure.

"You're gonna get killed!"

"Tony, I'll be fine…"

"Do you have any idea what you're doing?"

"Yes. I've done it before."

"What you're doing is crazy. You know that, right?"

"Yes. It's a bit nuts. But I'm better than you think. I'm a two-time Golden Gloves champ."

"I don't care. I don't want you getting in there."

"I'll be fine."

"If your opponent *kills* you, she gets to go home and have dinner—it's legal murder!"

"I won't get killed…relax."

"Don't tell me to relax. You're my *sister*. I already lost one. I ain't losin' another one."

"You won't lose me. Come to my fight. If you saw me box, you'd feel different."

"I will never feel different. I will never watch you box. You're in the hurt business. Don't you get that? The *hurt* business…"

"It's a game, Tony. It's a sport. There's a ref. If I'm in trouble, the ref will step in."

"Don't matter. People get killed all the time in boxing."

"*Stop* filling my head with fear…"

"It's the truth."

I TRIED TO KEEP Tony's words out of my mind for the sake of competition. With three days of fighting before me, I couldn't afford his negativity in my head before I stepped in the ring.

On day one, I faced off against Crystal, a woman in her twenties who had served in the Marine Corps and was in phenomenal physical condition.

Fuck! A Marine? went through my head. I thought about the grueling fitness training a Marine endures to prepare for real battle-related challenges, including crawls, grenade throwing, agility running, and dragging and carrying the wounded. Marines are trained to endure severe stress, trained to fight without panic, trained to overcome fear and pain in the most volatile circumstances.

At five foot ten, Crystal was lean and muscular with longer arms than mine, giving her the advantage from the start. I strategized before I stepped in the square with her, relying on my past experience fighting a tall girl. During the first of three elimination fights, few people filled the audience. Knowing I might lose, I was comforted to see a tiny crowd of boys and men, who, like so many times before, came to see the girls fight.

Robert, who was working my corner that day, said few words before the starting bell.

"You know what you have to do."

"Yes…slip her punches. Bob and weave until I see an opening. Then strike."

"Come out with your jab. Hard and fast. If you gotta take a few shots to get in, take 'em. When she feels your jab, she'll back off."

"This girl is a *Marine.*"

"Don't think about that. She's human. She can fall."

In round one, Crystal imposed her strength quick, punching me first with a left-right-left combination. My instincts told me to back away from the pain she imposed, but I moved forward, stood my ground, and took her punishment.

"Jab! Jab! Jab!" Robert screamed.

My left arm shot five jabs in a row, like bullets from a gun. The crowd rose to its feet.

"Holy shit!" yelled a man in the audience. "You broke her nose!"

The damage I caused took a few milliseconds to process. My jab worked, forcing a gush of dark red blood to stream down her lips and chin. She didn't know how to block my jab, so I pummeled her with the same shot, over and over again, rarely using my hard right. Crystal seemed oblivious to the blood, and outpointed me early on, costing me the first round.

"Fuck. She's winning," I said, out of breath, in my corner during the rest bell. "This girl is strong."

"It's okay," Robert reassured. "She's already getting tired. You'll take the second round. Keep that jab goin'. Your shots to her face are working."

In round two, I followed Robert's orders, and pummeled her nose. The crowd went wild, with teenage boys lining up at ringside to get a closer look at the bloody brawl.

"Again! Again! Hit her in the nose again!" one screamed.

Every time I threw my jab I connected with her face. This punch forced more blood to spatter through the air, onto the ring mat and into my face, and I winced when a foreign taste on my tongue entered my mouth. But Crystal fought like a champ, outpointing me again in the second round. The exhaustion from taking her punches left me depleted, and I wondered how much longer I could take her punishment. Robert looked concerned when I went back to my corner for my second rest before the last round.

"She's still winning," he told me.

"I know…"

"Are you bleeding?"

"No. It's her blood."

"Are you hurt?"

"No. But I'm tired…so tired."

"Okay…deep breaths. Only two more minutes. You can do this. You can finish."

I looked over Robert's shoulder to Crystal's corner. Her trainer held her nose in a blood-drenched towel in a failed attempt to slow her bleeding. I still wanted the win, but at the same time, I worried about the physical state of my opponent, and how much longer the ref would allow the fight to go on.

"They need to stop this fight," I told Robert. "She's really hurt."

"That means you still have a chance."

In round three, Crystal came out as strong as she did in round one. Her nose broken and blocked by blood and swelling, she breathed through her mouth, puffing with sprays of red filling the small space between us. About thirty seconds later, the ref stepped in, stopped the fight, and sent us both back to our corners.

Robert smiled when I asked: "What just happened?"

"You won."

"I *won*?"

"By TKO. Her corner threw in the towel."

"Holy shit…I didn't expect that to happen."

I remained in disbelief until we were called to the middle of the ring, and the referee raised my hand as the winner. He then instructed Crystal and me to see the doctor on-site immediately.

"Great fight," the doc said while pointing a penlight into my eyes. "How do you feel?"

"Okay. But her blood got in my mouth. Should I be worried?"

"No. You're fine. It happens all the time in boxing."

"What about disease?"

"The chance of getting a virus is slim to none."

"That's not very reassuring."

"Don't worry. The two of you already cleared the physical to box. You're both healthy. You're fine. Enjoy your win. You earned it."

Later that afternoon, when I returned home to rest, the elation of winning my first fight out of three was fleeting. Exhaustion consumed me, my body tired and aching, and my mind filled with anxiety over my second fight the very next day. I slept restlessly, knowing my body didn't have time to fully recuperate. But I also knew the power of mind over matter. I pushed the physical pain out of my thoughts and focused on my next battle in the square.

On day two, I went toe-to-toe with Jaime, a stocky boxer in her late teens whose spirit exuded meanness the moment we locked eyes. She brought a posse with her who sat ringside, and snickered about me within earshot, making old lady wisecracks that failed to rattle me. Coach worked my corner, keeping me grounded and focused on the task at hand.

"You know that's a sign of weakness, right? People always talk smack when they're scared. They're trying to tear you down."

"I know. I'm used to it. I just wish it were different. I wish we could support each other. Show a little sportsmanship. Show a little respect. Woman to woman."

"That's not the way it works. There will always be people out there trying to break you. Even the most remarkable people on earth have haters."

"I heard she's pretty tough. What do you know about her?"

"She's young. Immature in the ring. She's gonna come out swinging. Take your time. Save your energy. Let her tire out, then pick your punches. Hit her hard with your jab, and follow up with your hard right. That'll slow her down."

Coach's premonition was right. The moment the bell rang, Jamie charged out swinging a flurry of punches, failing to connect with blows to my face and body, making her tire out quick. I picked my shots with accuracy, throwing half as many as Jaime, earning points every time. This fight felt like child's play compared to my match the day before against the Marine. Jamie's punches inflicted no pain, and I realized her bark was worse than her bite. By the end of round one, she was already spent, and I walked back to my corner, barely breaking a sweat. I hoped to sit on my stool and take a quick sip of water, but there was no seat in sight. Across the ring, Jaime's cornerman sat her down on a stool, where she heaved and tried to catch her breath.

"Where's my seat?" I asked Coach through my mouthpiece.

He ignored my question, gave me a sip of water while I was still standing, and pulled me close to say something in my ear. I thought he was going to tell me the strategy of my next move.

"Why was Cinderella so bad at baseball?"

I looked at him confused.

"Huh? Why?"

"Because she had a pumpkin for a coach."

His baseball joke made me laugh out loud.

"Coach, where's my seat?"

He ignored my question again and responded with another joke.

"Why was Cinderella taken out of the game?"

"Why?"

"Because she ran away from the ball."

When the bell rang for round two, I was still laughing when Jaime came toward me. Her punches lacked steam behind her exhaustion and visible frustration.

"Jab! Jab! Jab!" Coach yelled.

I executed, forcing Jamie back, and followed up with my hard straight right, forcing her to halt. The referee stepped in and stopped the fight, and told us to go back to our corners. This time, my stool was in place.

"Good job," Coach said calmly. "How do you feel?"

"Great. That was quick."

"Yes. I knew it would be."

"Why didn't you give me my seat before?"

"If she saw you standing between rounds, she'd think you didn't *need* to sit down. You already beat her physically. We wanted to beat her mentally."

"Was the joke part of the mind game, too?"

"Yes. When she saw you laughing, she thought you were invincible. Remember, boxing is ninety percent mental, ten percent physical."

When the referee called Jamie and me back to the center of the ring, she wasn't happy when he raised my hand as the winner by technical knockout. Elation consumed me, not only because I won, but because I won in the face of her pissed-off fans.

"We're not done yet," Coach said as he escorted me to her friends with angry looks on their faces. One by one, he made me shake their hands. Several refused to make eye contact with me, but with Coach standing at my side, they reluctantly followed suit.

"Why did you make me do that?" I asked Coach later.

He smiled and didn't respond, with wisdom behind his eyes that words can't convey.

That night, once again, I couldn't rest. I won two fights, back-to-back by technical knockout, but instead of feeling on the top of the world, I thought about the next day, and worried if I'd have the energy and strength to win again. The last day was the finals, the biggest day of the tournament, where hundreds gathered to see the best of the best who made it through. That morning, I saw my competitor, Kristin, who looked scared when we locked eyes. I stared her down with a glare, forcing her eyes to turn away, and I believed I defeated her mentally before the fight. Like the two opponents I already beat, this girl was younger than me. She appeared meek and shy, giving me a false sense of security before we stepped in the ring.

When our names were called to fight, I walked into the recreation room down an aisle toward the ring. My nervousness soared at the sight of so many people in the audience, filling all the seats, with many in standing room only. Robert was working my corner, along with Layla, the young woman who cost me a standing eight at my first exhibition, the young woman who beat me at my first amateur fight.

"How do you feel?" Robert said in my corner as she poured water into my mouth.

"Good. But I'm so tired…"

"I know. Remember, she fought two days in a row, too. She's tired, too."

"What if she gets lucky with a knockout?"

"Don't think like that. She won't knock you out. You'll do great. No matter what."

The last thing I wanted was defeat after two days of winning. I prayed Robert was right, that my opponent was just as tired as I was, but I was wrong. When the first bell rang, we charged toward each other, throwing flurries of combinations. My nose-breaking jab failed to slow her down, and she outpointed me three to one. This seemingly shy little girl wasn't meek. She possessed strength, endurance and confidence, and dominated that ring. When I went back to my corner, Robert tried to encourage me, even though it was obvious I was losing.

"You're doing fine. Keep that jab up. Only two more rounds to go."

"My arm feels like a ton of bricks. I have no power."

"Focus. Give it everything you got."

In round two, Kristin came out even stronger, scoring quick with her jab to my eyes, hard right to my gut, and left hook to my face. When I tried to catch my breath, she battered me again with her perfect combinations. I became dizzy, and for the first time since I started boxing, was overcome with fear that I was going to get knocked out. I felt relieved when the second rest bell rang, knowing I only had one more round to go. Robert continued being supportive, even though I was getting my ass kicked.

"Just breathe. You're okay. Breathe…"

"I don't know if I can take another round."

"Yes. You can."

In round three, I knew my only chance at winning was to knock Kristin out. But I couldn't think about the fight anymore, just the remaining seconds until it was over. When the final bell rang, and the crowd gave us a standing ovation for putting on a great show, my heart sank. Kristin won, beating me by three points.

After we left the ring, I found an empty room on-site, where I sat alone in a corner and cried. I berated myself for working so hard to prepare for this tournament, only to lose. I beat myself up for failing in the finals, believing I might have won if I had more time to heal and rest. When I left the room, outside in the hallway, a small crowd of girls, including boxers from other weight classes I didn't fight, waited for me. They said no words as they surrounded me in a circle, and embraced me one at a time. Layla worked her way through the girls, took me in her arms, and whispered in my ear.

"You're awesome. Never forget that."

16
TRANSFORMATION

"Subconsciously—I didn't know it then, I realize it today when I know a little bit more about the mind and the brain—I fought like I didn't deserve to live."—Jake LaMotta

Three days later, I returned to Kid Gloves to train. I feared I'd face ridicule for losing the finals, for losing steam in the last fight. Guys at the boxing gym razz each other pretty hard, and I was no different since I had earned a place among them. I walked through the doors prepared to take it like a man, and vowed not to shed a tear.

"Disaster Diva!" Robert yelled from across the room. "Welcome home, champ!"

The guys stopped mid-workout, surrounded me, and one by one, congratulated me.

"Great job out there," one boxer said, shaking my hand. "I saw you fight that Marine. Holy shit. What a show."

Another took his picture standing next to me.

"Can't believe you're back so soon. Ain't ya sore? Ain't ya tired?"

"Yes. I'm sore and tired as fuck. But I gotta get back to work."

"That's a true champ right there."

Robert pulled me away from the adoration, sat me on the side of the ring, got down on one knee, and wrapped my hands. He told me to warm up shadowboxing before hitting the heavy bag for four rounds.

"Then I want you to spar for three rounds."

"Three rounds? Robert, I'm still sore. Can I skip sparring today?"

"You already took three days off. Three rounds. That's all I ask for. Then you need to skip rope, and do your push-ups and sit-ups."

My disappointment over losing in the finals lifted with each moment of sweat and adrenaline, and by the time my training session was over, I felt calm and at ease. Robert was all about moving forward, reminded me the past is the past, and the only way out is through.

"By the way, you're fighting again in a month."

"So soon?"

"That's four weeks from now. I don't want you getting rusty. The sooner you get back in there, the better."

He signed me up to box in a small Southern California District Championship fight in Oxnard, just a few towns away from Kid Gloves in Simi Valley.

"I want you to lose six more pounds."

"Six more? I'm starving already. Why do I need to drop?"

"I think you'd do great in a lower weight class."

I cringed at the thought of eating even less. Still, I agreed, knowing I had the strength of mind over matter. My body was resilient enough to whittle down thinner, and still have the strength and stamina to fight. But I didn't expect the toll this added weight loss took on my emotions. I felt raw from hunger that fueled my empty-bellied crankiness, and I lashed out against people closest to me, primarily Robert. But he never snapped back.

"Transfer that anger into training. When you're mad, hit the bag harder, run faster, skip another round of rope. It helps. You'll see."

He was right. After each training session, I was too tired to feel any emotion at all, until the next day came around, and I'd have to go through it all over again.

IN THE BEGINNING of my journalism career, I strived for the coveted spot of my byline on the front page above the fold. This mindset lasted for years, and I reached my goal time and time again, always getting an edge over other journalists in town, which, at the time, were many. Every time a big story hit Simi Valley, reporters swarmed in media frenzy from the *Los Angeles Times*, *Los Angeles Daily News*, and television stations. Face to face, we were cordial, but deep down we fought for the best story, boosting our already inflated egos in the newsroom. Even though I worked at the *Ventura County Star*, which was small in circulation compared to the metropolitan competition, I almost always nabbed the best story, gathering that one detail, or that one photograph, that nobody else could access. But something inside me changed from my early days as a reporter. I began to soften. I started to care about how my stories affected people when they read them.

This turning point occurred when I went out on assignment to write about a little boy, Joel, a second-grader who went missing in Moorpark, a small town just a few miles away from Simi Valley, where everyone knew everyone on some level. This community of less than 100,000 people was home to mostly families, who resonated to the area's top schools in Ventura County, and the fact that Moorpark had its own police department, making it one of the safest cities in the nation. Joel went missing on his way home from school, and when he didn't return, the entire town went on high alert to find his whereabouts. Everyone, especially Joel's family, thought the worst: that someone abducted the blond-haired, blue-eyed boy, and done the unthinkable. When I went out on the scene, a swarm of television media surrounded Joel's house, along with numerous police cars, and my competitors from rival newspapers. My photographer was waiting for me on the sidewalk outside, and cops stood at the front door of the sequestered family to prevent reporters from badgering. Children from nearby homes surrounded the scene, rode their bicycles and skateboards, charged by the excitement that brought focus to their tiny neighborhood. My photographer and I were competing against all the journalists on site, and knew there was one thing that nobody else had: Joel's photograph.

"We need a picture of Joel," I said loud enough for the children within earshot to hear.

A little boy riding by on his bicycle heard me, and stopped.

"I have a picture of Joel."

"Really? Where is it?"

"In my house… I can get it for you."

The boy was Joel's little brother, and too young to understand the magnitude of what was going on—that his big brother was missing, that we were there to report this horrible tragedy. I looked at my photographer, who appeared shocked at what the child offered to do for me, and waited for my response.

"No, sweetheart, that's okay."

In that moment, I no longer cared about having an edge, getting that extra detail, landing on the front page above the fold. I knew if I allowed this boy to retrieve his big brother's photo, not only would his family be enraged, but at some point, that child would grow up. Most people hate the press anyway, and when that child became a man, he would remember the insensitive, thoughtless reporter who asked him to retrieve his brother's picture in the midst of his family's trauma. My story ran the next day on page three, and I didn't care. My heart went out to the family, who soon discovered what really happened to Joel. He was walking home from school, like so many times before, and took a short cut across the Arroyo Simi, a westward-running creek that spanned from the city of Simi Valley through Moorpark. Rain poured nonstop in the days prior, making the rocks slippery. Joel lost his footing, hit his head and drowned, and water carried his body down the creek. Coroners determined Joel died instantly, which brought a slight relief to his parents, knowing Joel didn't suffer, that nobody kidnapped him. Because of this story, my heart softened permanently, shifting my focus from being a cutthroat reporter to one with compassion.

Unexpectedly, the softening of my heart translated to boxing. I still desired victory in the ring, but the edge I needed to hurt my opponent faded. I knew I needed this edge to not only win, but prevent getting hurt, by whoever wanted to take me out.

ON THE DAY of the Southern California District Championship fight in Oxnard, few fighters showed up, boys or girls. Robert believed I would win no matter what, adding another notch to my boxing record. As I walked around looking for my opponent, I saw two girls with heavy frames, and knew they weren't in my weight class. The boxing officials then informed us no girl showed up who matched my weight, meaning I took an automatic win through something called a walk-over. On the books, I was now the 1999 Southern California District Champion, giving me three championship titles since I started amateur boxing.

On the ride back to Simi Valley with Robert, I sat in the passenger seat and scarfed down a bag of Cheetos like it was my last meal.

"Damn, you were hungry, weren't you."

"Hell, yeah. I've been eating less than 1,000 calories a day for weeks. No fat. No sugar. No carbs. This tastes like heaven."

Robert laughed.

"I get it. But take it easy. You can binge on that bag. But that's it. I've already signed you up for another fight."

"When? Where?"

"Two months. At the Hollywood Park Casino."

"What's the weight class?"

"134."

"That means I can gain a few pounds."

"No it doesn't. I don't want you sluggish. It's better to weigh in a few pounds lighter."

"Damn…well, fighting at the casino sounds cool. I've never fought at a casino before."

"It's different. Much different."

"How so?"

"It's a casino. There's booze. The crowd will be drunk. Mostly men."

"So we'll be objectified. Like the ring card girls."

"Probably. But who cares? If you win this fight, it's another W on your boxing book."

"Another W. It's all about the W…"

Robert looked puzzled.

"Don't you want another win? Where's your head, Disaster Diva?"

"I don't know. Not in the ring."

For my fight at the Hollywood Park Casino, I invited a few colleagues from the newspaper to watch. These reporters and editors were intrigued by my involvement with boxing, which, by that time, earned me quite a bit of press in local newspapers and boxing magazines.

"I've never seen a woman box before," one colleague told me. "Do you wear headgear?"

"Hell yes. Thank God."

"Good. You're a reporter…you need your brain."

"Yes. A scrambled mind is never good for writing."

"I'm shocked you box. I'd never peg you as a fighter. Someone out for blood."

"I get that a lot."

On the day of the match, I showed up for weigh-ins, and discovered who my opponent was—Lisa, the same girl I fought in Tulare, the girl whose nose I broke just a few months before. I still felt bad for hurting this girl, causing her physical pain. When Lisa saw me, her face turned white.

"Oh no. It's you again."

"Lisa, how are you? How's your nose?"

"Still healing. Please don't break it again. That really hurt."

"I know. I'm sorry."

"It's okay. It's boxing."

"Well, good luck."

"Good luck to you, too."

Boxing at the Hollywood Park Casino, like Robert said, was vastly different than fighting in a tournament, where coaches and trainers honed their fighters in a sober setting. The smell of booze filled the air, and the crowd was drunk and obnoxious, as we fighters warmed up and got our hands wrapped inside a back room. Lisa and I were the only girls fighting on a pro undercard. When we stepped in the ring, we heard whistles and catcalls, the men whooping at us in sloppy drunkenness.

"Take it off!"

"Get it on!"

"Where's your ring card?"

Robert saw the disgusted look on my face.

"Ignore them."

"I can't. They're disgusting."

"I know. Blow it off. You gotta focus."

The moment the first bell rang, Lisa came out swinging with combinations. I slipped and dodged her punches, threw a few back, and avoided hitting her in the nose. She outpointed me quick, earning a win in round one.

"What are you doing?" Robert asked in my corner. "Why aren't you hitting her?"

"I don't want to hurt her again."

"You don't want to hurt her? What's the matter with you? You're losing. And you know it. Where's your jab? You can take her out with your jab."

"I know."

"Then do it."

In round two, I held back again. With each passing moment, Lisa's confidence grew. Her punches failed to hurt me, but they connected, racking up points.

"Where's your head?" Robert barked in my corner after round two. "She's winning. You're gonna have to knock her out in round three if you want to take this."

"I don't wanna hurt her, Robert. I can't hurt her again."

"Then this fight is over."

17

MAKING HEADLINES

"Character is that quality upon which you can depend under pressure and other conditions."
—Cus D'Amato

I returned to the newsroom a little embarrassed after losing my fight at the Hollywood Park Casino in front of my colleagues. But I also felt good for not hurting Lisa again. This contrast created an inner conflict over my feelings about boxing, which I never discussed with my coaches. I still wanted to trailblaze in the sport for the girls who came after me, creating a space of equality and respect for them, but at the same time, my desire to compete was fleeting.

My colleagues greeted me with adoration, still buzzed with excitement from watching two women box.

"When are you fighting again?" a male reporter asked me.

"Not sure. But the Everlast Championships in Texas are coming up."

"Wow. I heard that's a big deal."

"It is. The best of the best women fighters come from all over the nation to box."

"So that boosts their credibility. Women in boxing."

"Yes. Women are still banned from boxing at the Olympics. So this is a good move for equality."

"Well, you are athletes, just like the men."

"Women still aren't taken seriously in boxing. We're objectified. People think we're a joke."

"Watching your fight was no joke. That was awesome. I've never seen women box before."

"Most people haven't."

"What do you think it's going to take? For women to get the same respect as men?"

"We have to keep boxing. The more of us who stay with the sport, the more we'll earn respect. But it's gonna take time…"

At the urging of my coaches—and believing I played an important role in the world of women's boxing—I registered to compete in the Everlast Championships, which required money to travel and book two nights at a hotel in Midland, Texas. The fundraising took four months, and Robert guided me through the process, based on his experience generating donations for his nonprofit, the Kid Gloves Boxing Foundation. Robert knew many businessmen with deep pockets in town who he approached about my cause.

"I found some guys who wanna help," Robert told me. "But they're gonna wanna see you spar, watch you train, before they write a check."

"Sounds like an audition."

"Exactly. They wanna know what they're investing in."

"That makes me nervous. What if I don't pass?"

"Don't worry. When they see you spar, when they see how hard you train, they'll make a donation."

Checks poured in from numerous people, including Randy Adams, the Chief of Police in Simi Valley, who wrote me a note: *"Congratulations on your boxing story! From outstanding police reporter to outstanding boxer! Best of luck in the national championships in Texas. Someday I hope to be able to watch you compete."*

I received money from my aunts and uncles, including the aunt who told me to lose weight after my failed suicide attempt. Along with her check, she wrote encouraging words: *"I'm glad that boxing has been such a positive part of your life and I'm really proud of you."*

Karen Hibdon, my editor at *Ventura County Star* who saw me lose my fight at the Hollywood Park Casino, made a donation and offered words of support: *"I hope you do well, but no matter the outcome, you can always be proud of giving it a shot and working and being totally dedicated to your own personal goal."*

Otto Austel, president of the Simi Valley Chapter of Rotary International, donated money despite how he felt about boxing: *"It might be an understatement to say that I was very surprised to see you involved in the sport of boxing. I am personally opposed to this sport, because the knock-out blow is a result of the significant trauma to the brains of the participants, which renders them unconscious. Although I do not support boxing, I do support you and am one of your fans and admirers. Alicia, you seem to be a very unusual introspective person, searching for purpose, meaning and how best you can contribute to the world around you. It might be strange to me that you found something in boxing that has real meaning to you—lesson in discipline, dedication and desire, but that's good enough for me and I wish you the very best."*

Jim Carper, a coach at Kid Gloves, enclosed a check inside a card with a picture on the front of two female boxers. Inside he wrote: *"I'm sorry that I can't be there to cheer you on and to support you, but know that you already won. Take no prisoners."*

My boxing career also reconnected my mom and me, and gave us a chance to communicate and mend our relationship.

Weeks before Everlast, I visited her apartment in the San Fernando Valley, where she made me a 300-calorie dinner of skinless baked chicken and fresh green beans. After I ate, she prepared my chest protector by sewing plastic oval-shaped cups inside the bra top I'd wear on competition day.

"You know how I feel about boxing," she said as she sewed.

"I know, Mom. You think it's the dark side."

"I still believe that. But I know this is important to you. I'll support you any way I can. If you need anything, I'm here for you."

"I've always needed you. Why now?"

"I know I haven't always been there. I regret what I've done to you. Taking you away from Colorado, not protecting you from your stepdad. I wish I could take it all back."

My mom's heartfelt apology fell on silence for a few moments before I responded.

"I'm a stronger person because of what I went through. That shit made me strong."

"I never meant to hurt you."

"I hurt you, too. I know I was a pain in the ass at times. Let's try not to hurt each other anymore. Let's figure out a way to move forward."

"If that means supporting your boxing, okay. I support you. I pray for you. But I will never watch you box. I won't watch my baby girl get beat up."

"I understand. Boxing's not for everyone. But you know why I'm doing this, right? Not just for me, but for all women who want to box. It's about equal rights for women. I'm part of a bigger picture. If anyone should understand that, you should. You grew up in a time when women were marginalized. Women weren't as important as men. Things have gotten better, but women still have a long way to go. We still have a lot of work to do."

"It's just the way things were back then. I did what I had to do to survive."

"You've always been a survivor. You didn't break. No matter what happened, you never let it break you."

"I did break. I just tried not to show it. I had to be strong for you and your brothers. I did the best I could as a single mom."

"And you did great."

"I don't know about that."

"We're all still alive—that means you did great. We're still here."

"Yes, you're alive. That's why I'm so worried about you boxing. I don't want you getting hurt. You've been hurt enough."

My dad and I talked on the phone and wrote back and forth in emails. I expressed my fears over fighting in Texas, where I'd box other champions like me. My dad put my fears at ease.

> Have confidence in yourself, no matter what the reputation is of your opponents, fight your fight, you don't see the opponent, you only see standing in the ring with the gold! When you win—knock-out, decision, don't matter, only that you win—then you own them, otherwise, they own you! And nobody, nobody owns our girl. Prepare yourself both mentally (concentrate) and physically (get pumped) Do visioning—see yourself winning—big! I love you with all there is. I've walked in your shoes—yes, there's nerves—this is good, it's the source of your power and strength. You have prepared yourself physically—reflection, quiet, visioning—that's the edge, you have this edge through discipline. See yourself winning—see yourself receiving the gold—for all you are and (against) all those who doubted you. You have prepared well—this is your strength—semper fi!! You don't think, or analyze, you only STRIKE, you only COUNTER,

you don't see the punch or the pain coming, you only see the opening for your devastating left hook. She's down, she can't steal your dream, your goal and the gold is yours. You have no fear because you are ready, because you have a cause, to say, nobody owns Alicia Karen Doyle. You don't get tired, you don't weaken, you're quick, you know their game, you own all your opponents. You're hit, you don't feel the pain, she's down, the gold is yours. You're tired, you don't feel tired, she's down, you own her, the gold is yours. I'm in your corner. All my love."

Boxing's New Phenomena: WOMEN

By Valerie Martinez Gutierrez

They come with pigtails, make-up, nylon hose or false eyelashes, but make no mistake about it, they come to fight. During the last 10 years female boxers have hit the professional fight scene in full force. Mia Rosales St. John leads the way for women fighters emanating from the Southwest. The former model has parlayed her good looks and hard punching to become one of the more popular female fighters to watch. But can she fight? Yes she can, as her numerous knockouts can attest. And there are others such as Lucia Rijker, the hard-hitting and fearsome Dutch fighter who makes Los Angeles her base. Few women dare to jump in the ring with Rijker. Another champion is Christy Martin, who recently recorded a devastating knockout win in the Ricardo Lopez/Will Grigsby undercard in Las Vegas. She stopped her opponent with a jaw-breaking hook in the fifth-round.

It's a new wrinkle in the boxing world, but after a few tentative years, boxing fans the world over are convinced that women can fight. According to fight promoter Bob Arum,women fighters are becoming a bigger draw. Three other women fighters who have already made their debut are Leila Ali, Alicia Doyle, and Melissa Garcia. Ali, the daughter of Muhammad Ali, had her opening on October 13, 1999 at Madison Square Garden in New York. She scored a riveting knockout and has scheduled a second bout, according to Paul Tamayo of Sports Placement. Alicia Doyle, who fights out of the Kids Boxing Club and trains with St. John, is someone else to watch for. Also there is Melissa Garcia, 105 pounds, from San Francisco, who has the looks of a model and a cheerleader. Probably because she actually is a cheerleader for the San Francisco 49ers. Garcia has a record of 3-0. And both Alicia Doyle and Garcia, will be featured in upcoming issues of **UPPERCUT** in the very near future.

So **UPPERCUT** readers keep a watch out for all women fighters, the newcomers on the block. They're looking to show the world what they can do and they bring a new element to battles inside the ring with their combination of power and beauty. In the next edition of **UPPERCUT**, the world of women's boxing will be explored in detail. Furthermore, a regular section will be devoted solely to women's women boxing in each and every issue of **UPPERCUT** magazine. Let us know what you think.

44 UPPER CUT MAGAZINE

Photo of me in the winter 1999 issue of Uppercut Magazine.

On the day of the fight, the *Ventura County Star* ran a story on the front page of the sports section, written by Loren Ledin. The headline, "*The right combination,*" included the sub head: "*BOXING: About to embark on her biggest challenge yet, Alicia Doyle has found that her voyage into the ring has aided her outside it.*"

> Alicia Doyle discovered more than a sport since lacing on a pair of boxing gloves for the first time two years ago. The 29-year-old woman says she found herself.
>
> "Boxing has shown me what I'm capable of doing. It's given me confidence and boosted my self-esteem. I never dreamed what was possible to achieve until I got involved with boxing. Basically, it's given me the courage to chase my dreams. It's made the challenges in the rest of my life seem easy."
>
> What began as an exercise in curiosity has transformed into a voyage of self-discovery that has allowed Doyle, a newspaper reporter in Simi Valley and a resident of Sherman Oaks, to practically reinvent herself, both as a boxer and a person. With a two-year record of 5-4 as an amateur fighter, Doyle is poised for her most stirring challenge yet in the sport of women's boxing. Beginning today, Doyle will launch competition in the 132-pound division of the Women's U.S. Championships in Midland, Texas. Doyle is among nearly 100 women participating in the fourth women's-only national amateur boxing championships to be staged by USA Boxing. The five-day competition will conclude with titles awarded in 13 weight classes. Doyle, who trains out of Kid Gloves Boxing Studio in Simi Valley, may epitomize the changing stature of women's boxing. Constantly evolving, still breaking loose from its image as a novelty diversion to men's boxing, women

fighters are shedding the just-a-pretty-face stereotypes to blossom as accomplished pugilists in their own right. The eventual destination for America's top women boxers? Maybe a spot in the Summer Olympics, beginning in 2008. At least that's the target date for advocates eager to see women's boxing become a medal sport in the Summer Games.

"That seems like a realistic goal," stated Melanie Lay, an official with the Southern California Association of USA Boxing. "There are some stages along the way, such as introducing it as a demonstration sport. But we're all ready to see it happen. The great thing is that there is a lot of good talent being developed in this country. A lot of people think boxing is just Mia St. John in a pink robe. We've got young women training hard who are becoming outstanding boxers."

Danny Ortiz, a professional fighter for 13 years and now Doyle's coach, echoes that sentiment.

"What you're seeing, just like the men, is a group of women fighters who are training hard and learning the art of boxing. The talent level is getting better and better and so is the demand. Almost every boxing card had to have a women's bout." That women boxers have come a long way baby is a testament to the old-fashioned grit and determination, right from the beginning. USA Boxing lifted its ban on women's boxing in October of 1993, only after Dallas Malloy—a 16-year-old girl from Bellingham, Washington—filed a lawsuit seeking the right to participate.

Doyle acknowledges this uphill battle women fighters still face in 2000.

"Women have to work harder in this sport because we are women," she said. "To many boxing people, we are a novelty. I've heard us called the freak show. It's almost like we have to be twice as good to be recognized."

Doyle, like most of her colleagues in the sport, hardly concerns herself with the critics. She took up the sport in 1998 largely to test her physical limits. Since then, Doyle has extended her boundaries to Star Trek limits. Visiting places in her psyche she hadn't gone before.

"Sometimes, it takes all of my will just to go to the gym for another day's practice," said Doyle, a staff writer for the Simi Valley Star. "This sport is all about building a foundation of strength. There can't be any negativity. It's like when you step into the ring against an opponent. With all your friends and supporters, you're still alone at that moment when you go toe-to-toe with somebody else."

She adds: "I don't see boxing as a violent sport, like many others do. It's a way to challenge yourself. I'm still a person who believes in God. I think I'm in this sport for a purpose."

Out of the ring, Doyle is regarded by intimates as a kind, thoughtful friend who cares about kids and always makes it a point to console vanquished opponents. In the ring, she can be a focused tigress.

"Alicia is so kind, so good-hearted, but I never worry about her when she fights," said friend and Simi Valley resident Cheryl Smith. "I worry about the other person in the ring. She is so incredibly determined, so incredibly disciplined that she is becoming hard to stop."

While boxing has taught her lessons about herself, it has also helped to remake her personal life.

Her mother, Patsy Kong, supports Doyle's endeavor even while she can't bear to watch her daughter being hit in the ring and has yet to watch her fight. Her father, Frank Doyle, is once again becoming a part of her life after being out of touch since Alicia's childhood.

Both credit boxing for playing a role.

"I definitely think it's helped us to know each other again," said Frank, who lives in Colorado and will make the trip to Texas this week to see his daughter compete. "It has given us a common bond and that has helped the process."

Staff photo by **Rob Varela**

READY TO RUMBLE: Alicia Doyle, who has a two-year mark of 5-4, fights in the 132-pound division in today's Women's U.S. Championships in Midland, Texas.

The right combination

Photo of me that appeared on the front page of the sports section in the Ventura County Star *on April 11, 2000.*

With a record of 5-4, including a mark of the 2-1 in the National Blue and Gold in September, Doyle is developing quickly as a boxer. Her coach, Ortiz, thinks she has merely scratched the surface.

"She had so much to learn, particularly in technique and attitude," he said. "But you tell her once, and she has it down. I can't believe how much progress she has made. Before, she was straight up and down, no movement. Now she knows how to dance and attack. She has a great chance to win this tournament."

Just like the sport itself, Doyle isn't sure how it will turn out. "I still don't know why I'm here," she said. "Whether it's to turn pro or to coach or to just grow up some more. It's been a great experience."

18

EVERLAST

"When you break bones, they heal up and come back even stronger."—Jake LaMotta

Flying to Midland, Texas, from the Burbank airport was exciting, but unnerving. I collected $1,500 in donations to make the trip and made headlines, putting pressure on myself to win. I wanted to prevail, not only for me, but for everyone who gave monetary support and believed in me. I also wanted to impress my dad and stepmom, who met me at the fight venue in Texas to report the story live at ringside for *The Frank and Patty Show*, a radio segment they aired from a station near their farm home in Strasburg, Colorado.

I had never seen Texas before. When I arrived with Ron Kinney, a former boxer who agreed to work my corner, we laughed at the size of Midland, where fewer than 100,000 people lived.

"This is the middle of nowhere," I told him as we checked into our separate rooms at a hotel surrounded by flat desert filled with tumbleweeds.

"You ain't kiddin—it's smaller than Simi Valley."

"And we're in the *busy* part of town. Looks more like a place you'd hide a dead body."

The day before the tournament, we went to the fight venue inside a recreation center for weigh-ins, and hoped to catch a glimpse of my competition. Unlike previous fights where men filled the check-in rooms, women dominated at Everlast, where females made up the majority of trainers and coaches. Ron was among a handful of men there, and scoped out the girl I'd face in the ring.

"I saw your competitor."

"What do you know?"

"She's the number one contender here. She ranked sixth in the nation last year."

"Fuck."

"Don't let that scare you. You're a two-time Golden Gloves champ. You've busted noses. I'm sure she knows."

"Yeah…I knew coming in here I'd fight the best of the best."

"Yes. That's why *you're* here."

Later that evening, my dad and stepmom arrived, and we all met for dinner at a small café in town. I made my weight that morning, 129 pounds, and Ron gave me permission to eat.

"You can get a steak, a baked potato and some salad, but no dressing. And no bread and butter. I don't want you sluggish in the ring."

"What about pie?"

"Hell, no. You can get dessert after the fight."

Ron and my dad had much to talk about, as two former boxers. They both felt like father figures as they talked about me like I wasn't there.

"Alicia's doing great," Ron told my dad. "She trains like a beast. Harder than most men I've worked with."

"How's her footwork?"

"We had to work on that. She didn't move enough. She's got strong legs, so she'd just stand there, take punishment. I had to remind her every time she got punched, her opponent got the point."

"How's her endurance? How's her stamina?"

"Incredible. Especially when you think of her age."

"I'm glad she's got you in her corner. You seem like a good man…looking out for her well-being, her safety. You must have a daughter."

"Yes."

"Then you know…"

"Yes, I know."

The next morning, I grabbed my gear and headed for the fight venue, where my opponent arrived, ready to fight. Many fans showed up to support her, outnumbering my small group, and I heard through word of mouth she was an elementary school teacher. About an hour before fight time, my dad and stepmom sat ringside, where they set up their radio equipment to report the match live on air. My stepmom was on her cell phone with Tony, who asked to speak to me before I stepped in the ring. I was reluctant at first, and worried he'd fill my head with fear.

"How do ya feel?"

"Nervous."

"It's okay. That's normal."

"I know too much about her, how good she is."

"Believe me, she knows about you, too. She's just as nervous as you are. Keep your head up. Stand strong."

My opponent's stature reminded me of the stocky girl I beat by technical knockout on day two at the National Blue & Gold tournament. I strategized to throw my jab to rack up points, slow her down, bust her nose, and knock her out with my hard right. When the announcer called our names to step in the ring, the crowd went wild, like we were the headliner fight. The ref motioned us to the center of the ring, told us to protect ourselves at all times, as my opponent and I stared into each other's eyes. Back in my corner, waiting for the first bell to ring, Ron said few words.

"Okay, kid. Time to kick ass."

She came out swinging, forcing me to hold up my gloves and protect myself, nearly preventing me from throwing any shots. Her arms moved so fast, I assumed she'd waste her energy early on. I took her punches knowing I'd lose round one, and believed I could knock her out in round two. Her punches inflicted no pain, but felt annoying, like I was swatting away a cloud of flies. This lack of agony gave me an overinflated sense of confidence that I could win this fight. The moment she stopped throwing to take a breath, I hit her as hard as I could with my jab, stopped her in her tracks, and watched her stumble backwards.

I got her, I thought to myself.

When the rest bell rang, I walked back to my corner barely breaking a sweat.

"She's outpointing you."

"I know. I'll take her down in round two."

"Better do it fast. She's got too many punches on you."

"They don't hurt."

"Doesn't matter. She *knows* how to win."

Round two went by in a flash. For the first thirty seconds, her arms made me think of a windmill as she swatted my body and face with sloppy punches. I hit her again with my jab, forcing her to stop and stumble backwards once again. The referee stepped in, stopped the fight, and sent us back to our corners.

"What's going on?" I asked Ron. "Is she getting a standing eight?"

"I don't know...I didn't see that coming."

For a moment, I thought I won the easiest fight since I started boxing. But I knew something was wrong when her fans cheered on their feet. When I walked back to the center of the ring for the decision, the ref standing between my opponent and me raised her hand as the winner. I glanced over at my dad and stepmom, who looked dumbfounded. Ron seemed confused, too, when I asked what was going on.

"What the fuck just happened?"

"I don't know."

"Why did she win? How did she win? I thought the ref stopped the fight because she got hurt."

"Me too."

"This doesn't make any sense."

"I know. Lemme find out…"

Ron spoke to the judges, who told him I lost because of the fifteen-point rule, a rule I never knew about. When an amateur boxer racks up fifteen points over their opponent, the fight is automatically stopped. This rule is in place to prevent anyone from getting hurt.

"That sucks. I wasn't even tired."

"I know you weren't. I thought you had her."

"So she beat me by technical knockout?"

"Yes."

"I can't believe this…when I go home, the press is gonna say she knocked me out. Everyone's gonna think I got my ass kicked."

"Yes…but we know the truth. This sucks. But stuff like this happens all the time in boxing. You gotta take the loss and move on. There's nothing you can do about it now."

After the match, my opponent approached me with sportsmanship.

"I heard about you. When you hit me with your jab, I thought you broke my nose. You scared me."

"You didn't seem scared. You never stopped throwing punches."

"You know I had to do that, right? It was the only way to win."

"Yes, I know now."

"You're awesome for being here. We're both awesome for being here. Win or lose, this is a big deal for both of us, for all us girls here."

"Yeah…I'd feel better if I won."

That night, my dad and stepmom met Ron and me for dinner at the same café, where I ordered a quarter-pound cheeseburger with fries, an extra side of bread and butter, and hot apple pie topped with vanilla ice cream.

My dad saw the depth of disappointment on my face, and tried to shake me out of it.

"You've ruminated too long. Stop."

"I still can't believe it. I have to go home now and tell everyone I lost."

"So what? You still fought in the biggest women's boxing championship on the West Coast."

"But…"

"No buts. Stop that. I'm sick of it. This attitude is ugly on you. That's not who you are. Remember who you are."

"Where do I go from here?"

"I think you're done with amateurs. You boxed in there, took time to think, picked your shots like a pro. You outclassed her."

"She still won."

"She knew the rules as an amateur. That's why she won. You're a better fit for the big leagues."

"The pros?"

"Yes. I think you'd be great as a pro."

His words fell on a few moments of silence.

"Dad, I'm sorry I disappointed you today."

"You didn't disappoint me, baby girl. We're so proud of you. That was the most exciting thing we've ever seen. No matter how far you go in boxing, we'll be proud of you, no matter what."

The next morning, we all went our separate ways. On the plane ride home, Ron and I spoke about my next move.

"I agree with your dad. The pros are the next best step. You've outgrown amateurs."

"That sounds scary. It's dangerous. There's no headgear. The gloves are only eight ounces. I heard it feels like getting punched with a bare fist."

"Don't think about that now. Go home. Get some rest. Eat what you want for a couple of days. But not too much. Then get your butt back in the gym."

19

WHY AM I HERE?

"You can't think about the past anymore."
—Jake LaMotta

Returning to Kid Gloves forced me to face everyone who sponsored my trip. The *Ventura County Star* published a follow-up story about my loss, stating the simple facts: I lost the fight in round two when the referee stopped the contest, giving my opponent the win by technical knockout. The reporter who wrote the story couldn't interject his personal feelings in the article, but offered encouragement when I showed him the video of my fight.

"You didn't look tired. You weren't hurt."

"I know."

"I'm surprised they stopped the fight."

"Me too…I'm still upset. Embarrassed."

"Don't be. You're too hard on yourself."

"I know. I have a tendency to do that."

I wrote a follow-up letter to those who donated money for my trip to Texas, and Robert posted the letter at Kid Gloves on a placard in the front of the gym:

Sometimes when you lose, you win. Even though it might not be apparent at first. As you may know, I lost in the preliminary bouts earlier this month in the National Women's Everlast 2000 tournament in Texas. My shot at the title ended when I was outpointed by Amber Gideon, the number one contender at the tournament, who ranked number six in the nation last year. Needless to say, I am saddened by the loss, which came after many months of hard training, discipline and sacrifice. I wanted so much to bring home the gold medal, not just for myself, but for anyone who dares to aim high and dream big. More than anything, I wanted to inspire and encourage others to reach for the stars, no matter what obstacles might stand in the way. Now, in the wake of my loss, I look for the blessing. After all, the journey is more important than the destination. It's what you learn going through it that counts. I realize now that being one of less than 100 participants in the tournament was, in itself, a victory. It was a victory to go toe-to-toe with a top female contender. It was a victory to participate in one of only four national women's bouts in history. Looking back, there is no doubt in my mind that I prepared the best that I could for this competition. More important than the physical training was the spiritual and emotional nurturing I received from my coach, Danny Ortiz, and my family at Kid Gloves Boxing Studio. Just as important is the support I received from my sponsors. Without you, I would never have had the opportunity to compete in Texas. You made my dream quest possible. After having a few days to think and rest, I realize there is nowhere to go but forward. You learn a great deal about yourself in defeat. It's easy to remain positive when you're always winning. But in defeat, you have to push yourself further, not just physically, but emotionally and spiritually. In boxing, as in life, you win some, you lose some. But sometimes, when you lose, you win.

LESS THAN A WEEK after Everlast, I decided to turn pro. Robert found a fight a few months away at a brickyard in Castaic, California, where my professional debut featured the only two women on the undercard of men's boxing matches. I learned early on about my opponent, a pro from the start who never fought amateurs, coached by her dad and brother, who won her first and only professional fight by knockout. In the press, I learned she was tough, and perfected her knockout punch to get the fight over with as soon as possible.

Ron trained me for this fight, alongside Robert's brother, Danny, who spent hours with me per day, Monday through Saturday, preparing me for the biggest fight of my boxing career. For this match, I trained like I'd never trained before. I woke up at four a.m., met Danny at a nearby park to run four miles, followed by fifty-yard sprints on the grass. I went home, showered, and drove to the newsroom in Simi Valley, where I worked for eight hours. After my shift, I changed into my workout clothes and drove to Royal High School in Simi Valley, where I ran up and down the stadium steps for an hour before I went to Kid Gloves. There, Ron and Danny kept up the momentum as they watched me hit focus mitts, the heavy bag, double-end bag and speed bag. After that, they watched me spar with the men and picked apart my mistakes.

"You're too flat-footed," Danny criticized. "You're not movin' around enough."

"You're not slipping," Ron added. "You're not weaving. That's why you keep gettin' punched."

"This is *too hard*," I barked back. "I can't think straight."

"Just breathe. Relax," Danny advised. "You're thinking *too* much. Just let it flow. Your body knows what to do."

Ron walked over to my sparring partner and told him to go harder.

"She's not movin'. You gotta crack her. It's the only way she'll learn."

Fatigue consumed my body. My sparring partner executed with a straight right to my face.

"Move!" Danny yelled. "Get out of the fuckin' way!"

In what felt like an out-of-body experience, I slipped automatically. My sparring partner smiled and attempted the same punch again. I slipped, he missed.

"You got it!" Ron bellowed. "Finally!"

After two hours of training at Kid Gloves, Ron and Danny let me rest.

"Great job today," Danny said smiling. "I know that was hard."

"Harder than it's ever been before. I don't know if I can do this. Fight pro. I don't know why I agreed to this. Is it too late to back out?"

Danny laughed.

"You can back out if you want. The question is, how will you feel if you back out?"

"Like shit."

"I believe you can do this. Ron believes you can do this. You train hard. You're in shape. You're focused. You still don't realize how good you are."

"But am I good enough for the pros?"

"We believe you are. But you gotta be the one to believe."

I signed the contract on the dotted line. I'd get paid $650 for this fight, which didn't equate to the imminent danger I'd face. Amateurs were safer, where I wore protective headgear and twelve- to fourteen-ounce boxing gloves. In a pro fight, there's no headgear, and the gloves are eight ounces. The lighter weight doesn't sound like much, but a few ounces are huge. This protective covering determined the pain I'd feel from a punch.

"What do eight-ounce gloves feel like?" I asked Danny, who knew from his heyday in boxing.

"Like gettin' punched in the face with a bare fist. Bare knuckles on bones and flesh."

"I've never been punched with a bare fist."

"It hurts."

"That's reassuring."

"I'm not here to reassure you. It *hurts.* But your body is strong. The stronger your body is, the better you can take a punch."

"I don't get it."

"The better condition your body is, the stronger it is, the more it can take a punch. A punch to the face isn't just to the face. The whole body absorbs it. That's why boxers train so hard, to condition their body, make it strong to take any punch. You train harder than a lot of the guys I know. That's why I know you can take a punch. Even in a pro fight."

Ron and Danny tried to prepare me as best they could, but there was no way to prepare for the punishment in a professional boxing match. This training was more grueling than any fight I ever trained for in the past. My coaches took me to other boxing gyms throughout the San Fernando Valley and Los Angeles to spar with champions and retired fighters, all men. Outside of the gym, I felt like Rocky Balboa, with roadwork starting before the sun came up on the steep hillsides of Rocky Peak, a national park on the edge of Simi Valley, with forty-five-degree inclines stretching up for miles, forcing my lungs to expand to the point of pain with every gasp of air. To condition my legs, Robert made me do drills in the parking lot, where he affixed a harness to my upper body, attached to a Ford truck in neutral, and made me pull the vehicle forward with inertia, using every ounce of strength in my glutes, calves and thighs. This entire time, I ate 800 calories a day consisting of egg whites, grapefruit, skinless baked chicken and broccoli, with oatmeal at breakfast time as the only carbs allowed. Occasionally, my coaches gave me permission to eat a little bit of fat, five raw almonds, when they saw the toll the diet and training took on my emotions. At times, I was vulnerable, and cried for no reason. A champion bodybuilder at Kid Gloves helped me understand why.

"You're raw."

"What do you mean?"

"Your cells are starving. Your brain is starving. You have an imbalance, no serotonin. That's why your mood is jacked."

"How do you know?"

"I go through the same thing before competition. I starve my body to get ripped. It works. I win. But it's a painful process emotionally."

"There's no way around it?"

"Yes. Mentally."

"I don't understand."

"The mind is stronger than the body. When you feel down, tell yourself it's because of what you're putting your body through. Remind yourself it's because you're hungry. Think about something else. Think about your match. Focus on the fight. Remind yourself you're doing this for the fight."

Managing my emotions, at times, was harder than pushing my body further than its natural limits. This, combined with the growing fear and apprehension of my first pro fight, left me crying alone in my car after training, and when I returned home in solitude to rest. One time, after sparring with Robert's son, he saw me leave the gym, my eyes filled with tears. He thought he hit me too hard with body shots, and followed me out to my car to apologize.

"Are you okay?"

"No. I'm not."

"I'm sorry I hit you so hard. But the harder it is here, the better you'll be in your fight."

"I'm not upset about that. I know you're helping me prepare for battle."

"Then what is it?"

"I don't know…it's just…hard. Why is it so hard?"

He looked me in the eyes, and embraced me.

"I know it's hard. Not many people understand how hard this is. What it takes. What it does to us."

"How do you cope with all this?"

"I take it one day at a time. I have good days and bad days at the gym. On the bad days, I tell myself there's always tomorrow to do better."

I received a lot of press leading up to my match, and an editor at the *Los Angeles Business Journal* asked me to write a first-person column about my upcoming fight, which published with the headline *Search for Truth Lands Her Inside Ring*:

> For as long as I can remember, I've been searching for answers. Why am I here? What is my purpose? How can I make a difference in the world around me? Strangely enough, I found those answers in the boxing ring. Yes, boxing—a world that was once considered the mightiest sport featuring the world's finest athletes, that has since been tainted by corruption. A sport that, despite its dark business side, is filled with athletes who want only to discover the best part of themselves. Boxing brought out the best in me. I stumbled upon the sport two years ago as a newspaper reporter for the Ventura County Star. I received a call from a community activist about a place called Kid Gloves, a boxing gym in Simi Valley for at-risk youth that was destroyed by El Niño rains. At the time, my view of boxing echoed the stigma attached

to the sport—that it's a brutal world filled with criminals, cheats and liars. But after writing several stories about Kid Gloves, my views changed. What I found was a hidden world filled with good-hearted, giving people free of prejudice; a place where courage, determination and self-discipline are inspired. Over the past two years, my passion for boxing has grown. After months and months of hard training, I have had 10 amateur fights, accumulating a record of five wins and five losses, with three wins by knockout. I am a two-time Golden Gloves Champion, earning the first-ever women's Golden Gloves title in my weight class in the 1999 Southern California District trials. More important than my titles are the lessons I've learned. With discipline, dedication and desire, anything is possible. With perseverance, nothing is out of reach. And no matter what obstacles might stand in the way, integrity, honesty and hard work will make any goal a reality. Now, I want to share with others what I have learned. Boxing taught me focus and dedication. I learned clarity of mind and how to manage my emotions. And I discovered my own talents and strengths through persistence and self-awareness. In May, I quit my job at the Ventura County Star to pursue a professional career in women's boxing. My first professional bout will take place September 16 at a brickyard in Castaic. Quitting my job was a difficult decision. I've been a journalist for more than a decade now, working for publications including the San Diego Union Tribune, the Los Angeles Times and Los Angeles Daily News. My most recent job at the Ventura County Star gave me a decent salary with benefits and security. It was the kind of job that, if I chose to stay for many years, I could retire from comfortably. But after some serious thinking and prayer for guidance, I realized there is no such thing as "job security." I realized the only security I have is within myself. With confidence, I have the power to take my life in whatever direction I choose. I have to admit, boxing is a grueling sport. The training alone for my first pro debut has made me contemplate quitting many times. First, there's the diet: a strict caloric regimen of protein, vegetables, fruit and very little carbohydrates. Several weeks ago, when I weighed 144 pounds, I signed a contract that stated I would weigh in at 130 pounds by fight time to compete in the lower weight class. In professional boxing, if a fighter weighs in any higher than he or she has agreed, the fighter will most likely be fined, and may have to pay additional fees that will come out of his or her "purse," or paycheck. Then, there's the physical training. For endurance, I run four miles a day, six days a week. For strength, I do push-ups and sit-ups. For power, I hit the heavy bag. My workout, which ranges from two to three hours a day, also includes skipping rope, hitting the focus mitts, shadowboxing and other conditioning techniques. Many times I wonder: Why am I doing this? For me, turning pro is not about the money. It's about unleashing my courage and will. Just like every woman now breaking ground into women's athletics, we are here for a reason. That reason is to show, by example, that we can do it. To show, through our hard work and efforts, that any woman can box, play basketball, play soccer—sweat the same sweat, bleed the same blood, cry the same tears of loss and victory—as well as any man. As women involved in sports, we have to try twice as hard, simply because we are women. To me, that is the greatest challenge. I want to show that I am more than just a woman. I am a fighter.

Publicity shot of me hitting the focus mitts with Robert Ortiz at Kid Gloves Boxing Gym in Simi Valley, California, in 1999.

20 ONE PRO FIGHT

"He who is not courageous enough to take risks will accomplish nothing in life."—Muhammad Ali

Leading up to my pro debut, I spoke to Tony from time to time, but our conversations were brief. He didn't like the idea that his little sister was stepping in the ring without headgear, or that the rules were much different in a professional fight.

"You know, the ref won't stop the fight if you're in danger."

"Thanks for the vote of confidence."

"I'm serious. This ain't the amateurs. The crowd wants blood. They wanna see a knockout."

"I won't get knocked out."

"You don't know that."

"I *do* know. My body is strong. I've trained for this. I can take a punch."

"It only takes one lucky punch for a knockout."

"There you go again. Filling my head with fear."

"I'm telling you the *truth*."

"Jesus, Tony. You gotta have more faith in me."

"It ain't about faith. It's about reality. What you're about to do is dangerous, seriously dangerous. You might not be the same afterwards."

"You're scaring the shit out of me."

"Good."

"Look, I know you're worried. But please don't do this so close to the fight. I gotta stay positive. I can't afford to be afraid. Not now."

"I *really* wish you'd change your mind. Back out. Cancel."

"I can't back down now."

"Why not?"

"I'm too far in. What would people think?"

"Fuck what people think."

"I've come too far. I've worked too hard. It'd be all for nothing."

"Nothing? You've won titles. You've beat girls bloody. You're in the papers. Ain't that enough? When's it gonna be enough?"

I failed to answer.

"I'm sayin' all this because I love you. *We* love you. You don't have anything to prove to anyone. I think you're tryin' to fill some void. Some empty space from a long time ago. You don't have to fight to fill it. You've been fightin' your whole life. That battle is over. You already won. Don't you get it? You're alive. You're here. You came through on the other side."

"I never thought about it that way."

"I'm your big brother. I'm here to tell you the truth. I'm just lookin' out for you."

ON THE MORNING of my pro debut, Danny and Ron drove me to the fight venue for weigh-ins, where I saw my opponent with her dad and brother, who would work her corner. She stood shorter than me, a pretty, stocky, young Hispanic woman, and her stature reminded me of girls I beat in my previous bouts.

"She doesn't look as tough as the papers say," I told Danny after the weigh-ins.

"Never underestimate your opponent."

"I'm not. I'm just sayin'...she looks like girls I knocked out."

"That don't mean nothin'. Don't take this lightly. You're tough. But so is she. And she's already fought pro. You haven't. You still don't know what it's like."

"But I'm prepared. You and Ron prepared me."

"Yes. But we're not the ones gettin' in there. When you're in the fight, you're on your own."

The Castaic Brickyard buzzed with electric energy on the night of my fight, where hundreds showed up to watch the brawls. Robert and my fans from Kid Gloves and a few of my friends filled the audience, to cheer me on. I felt like a celebrity when strangers approached me, asked for my autograph, and took photographs with me at their side. On the surface, I appeared confident, but deep down, terror filled my psyche. My opponent and I would go toe-to-toe to fight four two-minute rounds, longer than I had fought before. Three two-minute rounds in my previous fights felt like an eternity, and I worried if my body possessed the strength for one more. I knew the importance of a strong mind before stepping in, pushed those thoughts aside the best I could, and tried to keep my head in the game.

In the dressing room, Robert surprised me with a gift, a black silk robe with a hood to wear into the ring, along with black silk shorts accented with a broad white band on the waist. As I slipped on my protective breast gear, I thought about my mother, who carefully sewed the plastic plates inside as we sat in her living room. I remembered the worried look on her face while she held the needle and thread, knowing she feared for my safety.

For a pro fight, each boxer picks a song to play on the loudspeakers as they walk down the aisle on the way to the ring. I chose *Leave You Far Behind* by Lunatic Calm. When the announcer called our names to fight, my opponent entered the ring first, and the crowd went wild. Then it was my turn. As I walked through a sea of screaming fans, the lyrics blared: *I want to push it right over the line; the line that you draw as you draw me near; I want to leave you far behind.*

Me walking into the ring with my corner men for my professional boxing debut in 2000 at the Castaic Brickyard in Southern California. Pictured left is Danny Ortiz; pictured right is Ron Kinney.

I climbed into the ring, where bright lights gleamed and television cameras pointed my way. I looked over to the corner of my opponent, who beamed with confidence, with her dad and brother at her side. This fight felt different from the amateurs, like we were two superstars on stage getting ready to perform a blockbuster show. In that moment, I realized the seriousness of the situation. This was a pro fight, a *real* fight, winner take all. I had never felt this level of fear, consumed with terror that my opponent would inflict permanent injury. Minutes before the first bell rang, I wondered what would happen if I quit after round one.

Ron and Danny placed a stool in my corner, asked me to sit down, and prepped me. They rubbed a thin layer of petroleum jelly on my face and arms so my opponent's leather gloves wouldn't stick and tear my skin when she made contact. Ron picked up my water bottle and gave me a sip before rinsing out my black mouthpiece. Danny tugged at the strings on my boxing gloves to make sure they were tight.

"This is it, kid," Ron said, looking into my eyes.

"You know what to do," Danny interjected. "Remember, you trained for this."

I nodded in acknowledgment.

The referee motioned my opponent and me to the center of the ring, where the announcer introduced us to the audience, starting with her. The crowd roared when they heard her undefeated pro fight record, and cheered for me when the announcer proclaimed this fight was my pro debut. The referee stepped in and told us the rules.

"Protect yourselves at all times. Let's have a clean fight. Touch gloves. Back to your corners."

Walking back to my corner felt like slow motion, like an out-of-body experience. I heard the crowd chanting my name: Disaster Diva! Disaster Diva! Disaster Diva! The screams were so loud, I only heard four words of Danny's instructions.

"Be first to strike."

I walked straight into battle, into a world of physical pain I had never felt before, and have never felt since. Each punch to my face felt like a brick being thrown from three feet away. The force of her blows sent a surge of agony through my entire body, from head to toe. It's impossible to convey what getting punched in the face with a fist inside an eight-ounce glove feels like. The only way to know is to experience this punishment firsthand. I threw my shots, worked my jab and hard right, and saw by the grimace on her face my combinations hurt.

Round one of my professional boxing debut in 2000 at the Castaic Brickyard in Southern California against Lisa Valencia.

I wanted to quit thirty seconds into round one. The pain was excruciating, and exhaustion overwhelmed me each time I threw and took a punch. She got me good early on, outpointed me quick, and I thought knocking her out was my only way to survive, and get this fight over with. The moment she stopped to catch her breath, I hit her in the face with my jab and busted her lower lip, forcing a gush of blood to spatter in my face, cover her teeth and drip down her chin. The shot worked, so I used it over and over again. The crowd went crazy at the sight of blood, causing more excitement, like they were watching two female gladiators fighting to the death.

When the rest bell rang, a sense of relief washed over me. But I had three more rounds to go.

"Keep that jab goin'," Danny ordered as he poured water into my mouth, then over my head.

"She's too…fuckin'…strong," I heaved.

"You're doin' good…but you gotta keep your hands up. You're takin' too many shots."

My corner man, Danny Ortiz, puts an ice pack on my face in between rounds during my professional boxing debut in 2000 at the Castaic Brickyard in Southern California.

Before I had a chance to respond, the bell for the second round rang. Terror filled my soul, once again. I saw the crowd standing from the corner of my eye and they screamed at the sight of us throwing blow after blow after blow. My opponent's lip split and bled more each time I shot my jab, but every time I stepped in, she outpunched me three to one. I knew I was losing, and I couldn't figure out how to win. There was no time to think, just survive, stay standing on my feet. I failed to bob and weave, failed to slip her straight right and left hook, and took more excruciating punishment with each passing second. When round two was over, I didn't believe I had the strength or will to go for round three.

"You gotta *move!*" Ron barked at me in my corner. "You're gettin' hit too much!"

"I can't…I can't…"

"You can! You're thinkin' too much. Just let it flow. Let your body do what it's trained to do."

"I don't wanna go back in there."

"You can do this!"

In the beginning of round three, I was so exhausted, my legs felt like anchors as I moved toward my opponent. I was surprised I could throw any punches at all, but somehow, they kept flying. I thought I could make it to the end if I had a moment to rest, so I went to the ropes, leaned back, and held my gloves up to my face. I strategized in my mind that if I let her hit me, she'd tire out, and I would knock her out when I saw an opening. This plan failed. When my gloves were up protecting my face, she hit me in the liver with her hard right, and sucked the wind out of me. My instincts for survival took over and forced me to move forward, punching her with the one shot that worked—my jab—into her already busted lip. So much blood spilled from her face I prayed the ref would stop the fight. Then I remembered, this wasn't the amateurs, and fights aren't stopped for something so trivial. At the end of round three, I watched my opponent in her corner heaving, out of breath. Her dad and brother wiped the red from her mouth with concerned looks on their faces.

"You won that round," Danny told me in my corner. "But the fight is close. You're gonna have to win the last round to take it all."

"I think she's tired."

"She is. And she's hurt."

Round three of my professional boxing debut in 2000 at the Castaic Brickyard in Southern California against Lisa Valencia.

I prayed she'd throw in the towel. But when the bell rang for round four, I knew going the full distance was imminent. My opponent came out sluggish, breathed heavy through her mouth, and spurted blood from her lip each time she exhaled. Then the unexpected happened. My hurt opponent, in obvious pain, took a deep breath and charged at me, striking me in the right side of my face with a left hook. I felt shocked by her perfectly executed blow that forced my head to whiplash. I didn't know how to block or slip this punch, so she used it over and over and over again. She hit me with this punch so many times, numbness consumed the right side of my face. A sense of rage surged through my veins, and instead of moving out of the way, I stood my ground. I allowed her hit me as I screamed through my mouthpiece, "You can't hurt me! Nobody can hurt me!"

Boxer Lisa Valencia pummels me with her left hook in round four during my professional boxing debut in 2000 at the Castaic Brickyard in Southern California.

When the final bell rang at the end of round four, we fell exhausted into each other's arms, and remained in an embrace until the ref pulled us apart. As we walked to our corners, our eyes remained locked over our shoulders, filled with tears and a look of respect and admiration for each other. I knew I had lost. But I also knew what it took for this girl to take the win. She pulled every ounce of strength inside her to finish, and prevailed with the heart of a lion. But there was no winner or loser in this fight. We both won in the eyes of each other, in the eyes of the audience.

Before my pro debut, I planned a feast at my favorite Chinese restaurant, and looked forward to chowing down on deep-fried orange beef, sweet and sour pork, and fried sesame balls. But as I changed in the dressing room after the fight, and swapped my sweaty boxing clothes for a hot pink dress with spaghetti straps and uncomfortable heels, I saw my face in the mirror. I took such a beating, swelling overwhelmed the right side of my jaw. I could barely open my mouth, let alone chew anything. Speaking was also a challenge. My tongue, crowded inside this swollen space, made me speak with a slight slur.

When I left the dressing room, television and newspaper reporters waited outside, and my opponent stood there alongside her dad and brother. She and I embraced once again as bulbs from cameras flickered around us. I saw the aftermath of the beating she took from my punches, black and blue around her eyes, and a split lower lip where the blood started to coagulate.

"Great fight…great fight," she said as we hugged. "How's your face? You okay?"

Inhibited from my injury, I spoke few words.

"I'm fine. *You* okay?"

"My lip hurts. But other than that, I'm good."

A woman in the crowd approached me with awe.

"I thought you won that fight."

"Really?"

"Yes, especially in round three, when she looked like giving up."

"She didn't."

"I know. It was amazing. I've never seen two women box before. That was the most exciting thing I've ever seen. You both were amazing."

Reporters praised us with congratulations on our fantastic battle, and the tremendous show we exhibited as women. Lisa gave her interviews with poise and grace, despite her split lip. I knew I sounded strange, and looked like I was in a bar fight, but the reporters didn't call me out on the matter.

"We're here with Alicia Doyle, two-time Golden Gloves champ. Tonight we witnessed her pro debut in women's boxing against Lisa Valencia, who skipped the amateurs and went straight pro, winning her first fight by knockout. Tonight, Lisa won her second fight against Alicia. Ladies and gentleman, these two women duked it out like nothing I've ever seen before. This brawl was bloody, not for the faint of heart. This fight far outshined the men. Nobody knew who won or lost until the judges gave Lisa the win. Alicia…now that the fight's over, what's next? Will you fight again?"

"First, I gotta give a shout out to Lisa for putting up a great fight," I responded. "I thought I could take her in the last round. But that girl gave it everything she got, and deserves the win. What's next for me, I don't know. That was the hardest fight of my boxing career. I gotta give it some thought."

Less than a week later, our match was deemed The California Female Fight of the Year. A story about the two of us appeared in *Southern California Fightscene* on September 16, 2000, in which reporter "Boxing Don" R. Dinkins wrote a rave review:

> Man your battle stations (or is it woman your battle stations?). Hide the kids and put up the LV rating (lots of violence), a war was about to break off. Chino's brawling, hard-punching, daddy-trained Lisa Valencia stepped in to take on the aggressive gear (forward) Alicia Doyle. Valencia comes from fighting stock ("I only spar with professional men boxers"). Her corner is really a family affair, with her dad Jerry and brother Mark working things. Her dad also manages her career and is very excited about his daughter's career. Lisa had

no amateur experience. Unlike Doyle, who used to do some kick-boxing. Doyle was making her debut, and given their respective backgrounds, this was an even match. SCFS has covered a lot of ladies' matches, and if you ask me when was the last time we've seen one this brutal, I'd say "Let me think about it for awhile." Folks, this was brutally brutal. Lisa's mom, who hates her daughter boxing, must still be recovering from this one. Seriously, are women supposed to be this tough? Damn! Deah Lohuis, long-time boxing commission member (how many fights has he watched?), came to me after the war, and said "Don, (that was) easily, the women's fight of the year can you believe that fight?" It started with Valencia forcing things as usual. ("I like to try and knock 'em out early so I can get outta there"), ramming the slower, plodding Doyle with fast, hard punches. She wasn't missing much, but it was obvious early, that Ms. Doyle was here to stay, stay and fight. She soaked up all Lisa tossed her way, but only rarely would she back up too far. She was doggedly determined, and at the bell, the crowd was in a frenzy! Round two saw Lisa still hammering on Alicia, even rocking her world on occasion, but now Doyle was landing on Lisa as well. Lisa's nose started bleeding and she was getting a little lumpy around the eyes. Did I say these ladies were tough? Each time Valencia would get off on Alicia, Alicia bit down on her mouthpiece and surged forward, landing hard punches on Lisa's bloody face, all the while, getting out-punched five to three. Doyle has strong, sturdy legs and she wasn't about to get knocked off her feet, no matter what came her way.

Photograph that appeared in Southern California FightScene on September 16, 2000, after my professional boxing debut against Lisa Valencia at the Castaic Brickyard in Southern California.

In the third round, Lisa trapped Doyle on the ropes and tormented her with awesome combinations, up and down. But when she paused for one second, a thunderous right from Doyle snapped her hard back, sending blood flying. To be honest, I was starting to get worried about these two and what they were doing to each other. By now, both ladies' faces were battered, but quit? Oh no, none of that. I was glad when the final round started. As the two ultimate warriors (not women warriors, just warriors) touched gloves at the round's beginning and the crowd of 800+ stood and vented. I wanted to say "could you guys touch each other like that for the whole round and not hurt each other anymore?" Lisa found a new weapon at the start of this round, her left hook. Once, twice, three times, a lady hit another lady with a left hook. Doyle seemed shocked to be hit by the same punch repeatedly. Finally, she fired back with a hard body shot, sending blood flying from Lisa's mouth (I guess you don't need all the gory details) as the crowd stood again, giving up plenty props as these two punched each other right up to the final bell. And at last, they fell into an embrace of mutual respect, total mutual respect! Just writing this account of this epic battle gives me goose bumps remembering the way the battle was fought and the crowd responded. As the scorecards were read, I knew it wasn't a draw and I knew there was no loser in this one. Only two winners. Valencia won a hard earned decision. Afterward, SCFS spoke with both ladies. Lisa, "she was a tough girl, really tough and she gave me a great fight. I'm glad I won." Alicia, "Lisa is a great fighter and I'm honored to have had a chance to fight her and maybe we'll do it again." Folks, it gets no better than this. Finally, all but one, in the Valencia clan was able to relax. Mom, not to worry, I know it's tough, but your baby can handle herself.

Mucho Props, Baby-After an unbelievable war, Valencia (L) and Doyle are both glad it's finally over. Valencia won. Valencia's brother Mark (far left) and dad Jerry offer congrats.

Lisa Valencia and I congratulate each other in a photograph that appeared in Southern California FightScene on September 16, 2000 after my professional boxing debut at the Castaic Brickyard in Southern California.

21

BODY AND SOUL

"You know what's the greatest sin in the world? Hurting your fellow man."—Jake LaMotta

When I returned to Kid Gloves a week after my pro debut, I looked lopsided from the bulge on the right side of my face. The injury impacted my right inner ear and caused a plugged-up sensation that left me deaf. I walked into the gym exhausted and sore, with a bruised ego.

"Disaster Diva!" Robert yelled when I came through the doors. "What are you doin' here? You should be home resting."

"I know. But I was going stir crazy."

"Did you go to the hospital? Get checked out?"

"No."

"You should. Make sure you didn't get a concussion."

"I feel fine. I just look terrible. And I can't hear out of my right ear."

Robert gently touched the right side of my face.

"You'll be okay. The swelling looks bad. But that'll go away in time."

"I'm here to train…get my mind off things."

"No way. Your body's still healing. You need to rest. Take it easy."

"Robert, I don't know if I can do this again. That fight was *hard*. Harder than I expected. Plus, I got hurt. Real bad."

"It's okay if you don't wanna do this anymore. Boxing *is* hard, especially the pros. It's not for everyone. You've already got your titles. Nobody can take those away from you. There's nothing more for you to prove in the ring. You've made your mark."

"Boxing's been such a big part of my life. I don't know how to live without it."

"You *can* live without it. You don't have to fight anymore to find yourself. You can learn to be happy without it."

"What will I do with myself?"

"You'll figure it out. You always have. You always will. You've always been a survivor. That will never change. You don't need boxing to know you can survive."

Because I quit my job at the newspaper to go freelance, the camaraderie in the newsroom ceased. I stayed away from the boxing gym to heal, which left a greater void of person-to-person stimulation. For the first time in years, I was literally alone. The only voice I heard was my own dialogue running through my head, and this painful solitude forced me to reassess everything in my life up to that point. When I found boxing, I believed I had found a cure for my depression, insecurity and self-perceived shortcomings. But as soon as I stopped training at the boxing gym and quit the fight scene, all my insecurities crept up again. I realized boxing served as a distraction, not a cure, and I had to face my demons head-on without fighting. My mom remained a great comfort in my life during this transition.

"I'm so glad you're not boxing anymore."

"I miss it. Terribly."

"I never understood why you started to begin with."

"I loved it. It made me feel powerful, invincible, like I could take on the world, like nothing could hurt me anymore."

"Baby girl…hurt is part of life. That's how you learn, how you grow."

"Why does it have to hurt so much?"

"It's just the way things are. Pain is a part of being human. It's why God put us here."

"God wants to hurt us?"

"No. God wants us to learn. Being alive means suffering sometimes. But suffering makes us strong. Makes us better. Suffering opens our hearts, our minds, makes us see things differently, makes us realize how strong we really are."

"I don't know what to do with myself now. I feel so empty. I feel lost."

"Keep writing. You've always loved writing. And now you're freelance. So you can pick and choose the stories you wanna write. You don't have to write doom and gloom anymore. You can write what you want."

From that point on, I billed myself as "The Writer Specializing in Good News," only writing stories that made me feel good when I wrote them, and made readers feel good when they read my words. I focused solely on things that made a difference.

One of the first stories I wrote when I left boxing was a follow-up about Joel, the little boy in Moorpark who died after slipping on a rock crossing the arroyo on his way home from school. When I called Joel's mother to arrange the interview, she graciously invited me into her home, and updated me on what transpired since her son's death.

"A lot has happened since Joel died…our lives changed in ways we never expected."

"How so?"

"Well, for one, my husband quit his job with a six-figure income. He was always at the office, never home. After Joel died, the money didn't matter anymore...he wanted to be home with me, with his other son. He makes less money, but he's happier, we're all happier. He coaches our other son's Little League now. We all volunteer together for charities in town."

"What else has happened since Joel died?"

"We raised a bunch of money to build a bridge over the arroyo."

"Wow...that's huge."

"Yes. We're so proud of that. Everyone in the community pitched in. We don't want any other child to die when they're crossing the arroyo. The kids *know* they're not supposed to take that shortcut. They're supposed to take the long way around. But kids will be kids. So we had to do something."

"How are you coping otherwise?"

"It's hard. Every day is hard. I still cry when it rains. It was pouring rain the day Joel died."

"I'm so sorry. I know it's hard to talk about, to relive it by talking to me."

"It's okay. We're getting through it. One day at a time. And in a strange way, it made us better."

"How?"

"We realized what's really important. Spending time together. Loving each other. Being there for each other. We'll always hurt over Joel. That will never go away. But sometimes, tragedy can make you better. In a strange way, it makes you stronger. I wish Joel was still alive. But there's nothing we can do to change that. So we have to move on."

"What did you do with Joel's things?"

"Everything's still here. Exactly as he left it. Would you like to see his room?"

She escorted me upstairs to Joel's bedroom, where toys remained scattered all over the floor, a dirty shirt and jeans hung from the inside doorknob, and crayons and paper with scribbled drawings covered a tiny desk.

"He was such a messy little boy," she said with a slight chuckle as her eyes brimmed with tears. "I miss him so much."

I put my arm around her shoulder when we sat down on Joel's twin bed. In this space, we remained silent, until a hummingbird hovered outside Joel's window.

"I see that hummingbird all the time," she said, gazing out the window. "It's Joel's spirit…he never left us."

A MONTH AFTER my pro boxing debut, I occasionally trained at Kid Gloves, where I hit the heavy bag and skipped rope, but avoided sparring. I was surprised when a reporter from the *Los Angeles Times*, Reed Johnson, reached out to write a follow-up story about me, and spent hours at the boxing gym interviewing my coaches and trainers. He wanted to see the videotape of my pro fight, so I invited him to my bungalow apartment where we watched the match together.

Reed's story, which encapsulated all that had occurred up to that point in my life, ran on the front page of the Life section on a Sunday in the year 2000, with the headline: *Body and Soul; An ex-reporter takes up pro boxing to show what she's made of – and to slay her inner demons.*

It was surreal reading Reed's article about me, in which he beautifully wove together my life story, including the most painful pieces of my past. He highlighted the fact that a mere 47 out of 420 licensed boxers—amateur and professional—were women at the time, according to his research with the California Athletic Commission.

The article opened with his experience of watching me assess my pro fight on videotape, and wrote that I was "happily scrutinizing" myself throwing jabs at my opponent's split upper lip, but a look of disgust washed over my face when I saw a blond bombshell strut across the screen in between rounds holding up a ring card. "That's sending the message women are just about T-and-A," I told Reed when we watched the fight. He wrote that I saw myself as a "crusader for female equality," and that I picked an "unusual" way to prove my point, including quitting my job as a reporter to become a professional boxer, which he described as "a vocational path…mined with danger." He also wrote about my pro debut, stating it was "an exemplary brawl" in which my opponent won by a unanimous decision, and that I was among 400 women in America at the time who were boxing professionally.

I loved the way Reed eloquently wrote about my life, but felt extremely vulnerable when I read the story, especially the parts about my childhood. *The Los Angeles Times* had hundreds of thousands of readers in the year 2000—with the biggest circulation on Sundays—and knowing that complete strangers knew about my past left me feeling exposed. But at the same time, I hoped that sharing these parts of myself might make a difference in the lives of others who had struggled with similar adversities.

The most unexpected impact of Reed's article occurred when it reached my big brother—Matthew from my mom's first marriage—who I had grown distant from since he went off to college when I was a child still living in Colorado. Matthew called me out of the blue after many years of disconnect, and hearing his voice reminded me of all the times he had protected me when I was young. Matthew and I never discussed what happened to us as children, and for years I believed he didn't want much to do with me, the daughter of the man who unintentionally turned our world upside down.

"Hey Alicia, it's Matthew," he said when I answered the

phone. Matthew had always called me by my nickname, Toy, and hearing my three-syllable name roll off his tongue sounded odd.

"Matthew...how are you? Everything okay?"

"Yes. I'm good."

Then he got straight to the point.

"I wanted to let you know I saw the article about you in *The Times*. Mom mailed me a copy."

I didn't respond, wondering what he'd say next, because a tone of disappointment filled his voice.

"The reporter referred to me as your half-brother."

"Yes...he did. Reporters are all about accuracy. He was being accurate."

"Well, I'm really upset about that."

"Why?"

"Because I'm your *brother*," he said, his voice breaking. "I've always been your brother. I've never called you my *half*-sister. You are my *sister*..."

"I know, Matthew. I feel the same way about you. Please don't take it personally. The reporter was just doing his job."

"I know we don't talk much. I know we never talked about what happened back then...how we fought so much when we were kids."

"It's okay. It's painful stuff. No need to dredge it all up again."

"I wasn't there for you. I know you were hurting. And sometimes, I made it worse."

"We were *both* hurting. Trying to make sense of it all. We were just kids. What were we supposed to do?"

"I could have been more supportive."

"You *were* supportive. Especially when it really mattered. When shit got *really* bad, you had my back. I knew you loved me..."

"I'm sorry...for everything."

"No need to be sorry. You don't have anything to be sorry for.

You were a great big brother. You and Luke both…I love you both so much. I wouldn't have survived that time if it weren't for you."

"I love you, too. And I will always be there for you. No matter what."

22

CATHARSIS

"Don't count the days, make the days count."
—Muhammad Ali

In the months following my pro boxing debut, I focused on building my freelance business, adjusted to life without starvation, and found workouts that didn't leave me with black eyes, body aches and the fear of fighting. I never went to the hospital after my pro fight, and never sought a diagnosis or treatment for the injury to my inner right ear, which remained swollen from the inside out.

I found great comfort in three-hour walks alone around the Hollywood Reservoir, and long hikes through Chumash Trail and Rocky Peak, where the Chumash Indians lived hundreds of years ago in the dramatic rocky outcroppings surrounded by native plants, hummingbirds and butterflies. On occasion, in the early morning hours before the sun came up, I spotted a deer or mountain lion, and immersed myself in the quiet, where my thoughts cleared away from the ring. In this solitude of self-examination, I came to life-altering realizations. My fight was never in the ring, but inward, with myself, my ego, my past, my inability to forgive, my inability to accept and move on. The only person hurting myself was me. This epiphany was a triumph that

I transferred into my writing. I wrote about people who overcame great odds and managed to harness peace in their own lives, including Holocaust survivors, women who overcame heinous acts of domestic violence, and children with special needs who faced the world head-on despite their limitations. Their vulnerability brought me comfort, and during the brief time I spent with them, their stories revealed the most beautiful aspect of human nature—vulnerability—the commonality we all share, a great equalizer that connects us on the deepest level.

I was surprised when Reed from the *Los Angeles Times* contacted me again to write a brief follow-up story, this time for an article on the front page of the Southern California Living section that ran on January 1, 2001, in celebration of the New Year. My recap ran under the headline, *Their Year That Was*: *A look at where some remarkable people are now,* which featured updates on three individuals that had been profiled in the previous twelve months.

I was honored that Reed selected me, of all people, who "shone" in the *Times*' pages, and gave "a glimpse of the startling range of life" that had been chronicled in the newspaper in the last year of the second millennium.

He wrote that shortly after *The Times* first profiled me, my adrenaline still ran high after my pro debut, but shortly after, I realized my heart wasn't there anymore. He also captured my newfound wisdom perfectly.

"I lived a huge part of my life angry and resentful and unforgiving, and the sport relieves a lot of that," I told Reed during the interview. "Right now I can't imagine getting in the ring and hurting another person anymore. And it's a very peaceful feeling."

Me standing inside a rock formation at Rocky Peak in Simi Valley, where I took long hikes after I retired from boxing in 2000.

EPILOGUE: OUT OF THE BOX

"The man who views the world at 50 the same as he did at 20 has wasted 30 years of his life."
—Muhammad Ali

My boxing career doesn't have the typical fairy tale ending. I quit after my first and only professional match. I never won a world title or a championship belt in the pros. The crescendo of my story doesn't end with my arm raised victorious in the ring. My wins came after I left the roped-off square, when I had a chance to contemplate the lessons I learned in the fight game. These lessons, which transcended into epiphanies, are my greatest reward.

Now, into middle age, I know I will never be able to capture or mimic the elation I felt inside the boxing ring, the natural high I felt after a win, the adrenaline that rushed through my veins in a fight, the adoration that fed my ego before and during matches. The only way to grasp these feelings is to box again, but punching someone out doesn't align with who I am today.

The anger I felt decades ago, the aggression that fueled my fire in battle, is a dull roar. Yes, the anger is still there. But I've found other ways to cope—most importantly, the way I view the anger now and what caused my angst to begin with. This process involved taking a hard and honest look at myself, and I realized building this self-awareness is a lifelong effort, so I'm never really done. Challenges, setbacks and disappointments are a part of being human. I'm wiser from the incidents that I thought would break me. The fact is, I'm still here, and looking back, I realize my fight was never in the ring. The battle was with myself, my thoughts, my old paradigm. I had to make an inner shift; otherwise, I would have remained on that battlefield, forever unprotected.

After I quit boxing, it took years for me to find myself again by deciphering my journey in the ring, the serendipitous circumstances that led me there, and, above all, why I exposed myself to a world of hurt. After all the battles survived as a child, I immersed myself in the fight again as an adult, making the deliberate choice to expose myself to pain, once again. Yes, pain in the ring is different because boxing is a sport. But during the entire time I boxed, I knew my presence there ran deep. It was as though I was recreating the pain I endured in childhood through boxing, which gave me a place to express my rage, overpower my opponent, and command the control I never had when I was young. When I walked away from boxing, I had to find ways to transcend my anger, depression and resentment without the fight. I had to find my power in my own ring of life.

Still, boxing was a catalyst for my transformation—a sport filled with metaphors that helped me view my life differently. Boxing wasn't about fighting in the ring. It was about fighting my *self*. Pugilism wasn't about knocking out an opponent. It was about knocking out my inner demons of the past, facing my memories in the eye, and remaining fearless no matter how much they frightened me. The hardest part was learning how to embrace my darkest pain and love the broken parts of myself, and accept that some wounds can never heal. Rather, these wounds callus over, dulling the point of initial contact, serving as a reminder that survival prevailed.

When I was boxing, I believed I had found a cure for my darkness. But when I retired, I became fully aware that the sport was a welcome distraction from what I needed to confront. When I quit the sport, all my emotional pain from the past returned in full force. I no longer had the intensity of boxing to make me forget all I had gone through, and I was back at square one. But I came to a point of enlightenment that helped me establish coping mechanisms. Forgiveness was part of this process; it didn't make me forget what happened, but I knew if I didn't forgive, my anger would kill my spirit.

The hurt I transcended didn't come from healing bruises and injuries I endured through training, sparring and getting punched. Healing on a physical level was easy. Healing my heart, mind, spirit and emotions was hard, and a challenge I continue to overcome to this very day. The difference between then and now is that I embrace this challenge as part of the human condition. I've come to realize that being alive means suffering, and this suffering is a beautiful and normal part of being human.

A few years ago, I delved deep into Buddhism, a philosophy that resonates with me, and makes more sense than any religion I experienced in my younger years—even though I continue to be grateful for the Science of Mind teaching my mother introduced me to at age twelve. The Buddhists believe "life is suffering," and this teaching helps me navigate through life in an honest way. I'm not going to lie and say my enlightenment led to nirvana. I never reached a point of happiness, which I concluded is overrated. What is happiness anyway? Rather, I found a state of grace, which is far more poignant than happiness could ever be. As noted in Ephesians: *"For it is by grace you have been saved, through faith..."*

Grace is a state of being able to manage my emotions, feel my internal pain and let it flow until I come through on the other side. My past still creeps up on me from time to time, and knowing *the only way out is through* helps me cope. I also had to stop trying to push these feelings away, because resisting these feelings made them stronger. This reminds me of a quote by Carl Jung: *"What you resist, persists."*

When I'm triggered to remember something painful from my past, I allow myself to feel the hurt in all its glory until it subsides. The memory transforms, like watching pictures on a movie screen that are separated from myself. Sometimes, when I watch these moving pictures in my mind, it feels like those things happened to someone else. And in a way, they did, because I'm no longer that person anymore. It's almost as though I've lived many lifetimes as a different person in each life, all leading up until now. Today, I am the sum of all these parts. I believe there are scars that make us who we are, and without them, we wouldn't exist. I love the scars that made me, the pain that molded my character, the experiences and circumstances that created who I am. I've stopped wishing those things in the past didn't happen. It's pointless. I can't change history. I can only control how I react to the memories through detachment. By trying to push the memories and feelings away, I was denying parts of myself. I have to love the light and the dark, the joy and the pain, especially the pain, because the pain made me who I am.

After I quit boxing in 2000, I became a freelance writer, and have since earned a reputation as "The Writer Specializing in Good News." Journalism continues to be my passion and I find great inspiration in writing about amazing people who overcome great odds—much greater than anything I have endured. These people remind me that yes, life can be hard and heartbreaking, but with faith, perseverance and never giving up, life can go on.

Since 2000, I haven't sparred or stepped inside the ring for relief; instead, I take long walks on the beach near my home in Ventura, on the California coast, where I feel grounded from sounds of the waves crashing in the ocean, smells of the saltwater filling the air, and views of the deep blue sea. In this pristine and calm setting, I am filled with a sense of gratitude for the beauty that surrounds me.

Me working with the girls as a volunteer coach in 2020 at Kid Gloves Boxing in Simi Valley, California. Pictured left is six-year-old Cynthia Medina; pictured center is eight-year-old Teagan Ortiz. Photo credit Teresa Medina.

I am still involved at Kid Gloves, but not as a fighter. I'm a volunteer coach, mentoring boys and girls ages five to fourteen, teaching them basic skills like blocking, bobbing and weaving, and shadowboxing. Many of these children are from broken homes, and several live with daily challenges, like attention deficit disorder and attention deficit hyperactivity disorder. Some of them face bullying in school, and when they show up at Kid Gloves with black eyes or cuts on their faces, I can't help but wonder who hurt them in the outside world. Knowing the fragility of these at-risk youths is heartbreaking at times, but the moment they slip on their boxing gloves, I see their confidence soar, and I'm reminded why I'm there. The boxing gym is their sanctuary, a safe haven away from their troubles, the place where I can give them unconditional love. When I spend time with them, especially the little girls, I'm reminded of the little girl I once was, how vulnerable and fragile I felt so many years ago. The little girls of today are so different than I was: they are strong, resilient and fearless in a world with fewer boundaries; they can be or do anything they want, and manifest dreams that seemed nearly impossible for little girls like me who grew up in the 1970s. It's unlikely that any of these tiny girls will ever box in amateurs or the pros, but the door is open if they want to, including boxing in the Olympics, which made women's boxing an official part of the Olympic Games in 2012. And meanwhile, the skills they learn in boxing will make them strong—giving them all a fighting chance.

It worked for me.

Portrait taken by Kathy Cruts in 2020.

ABOUT THE AUTHOR

Alicia Doyle is an award-winning journalist who discovered boxing at age twenty-eight in the late 1990s when she went on assignment at a boxing gym for at-risk youth called Kid Gloves. For two years, she simultaneously worked as a newspaper reporter while training and competing as a boxer, making her one of only a few hundred women in America at the time who infiltrated this male-dominated sport. During her boxing career, she won two Golden Gloves championship titles and earned three wins by knockout—and her pro debut at age 30 in the year 2000 was named The California Female Fight of the Year.

A journalist for more than two decades, Alicia has earned a reputation as "The Writer Specializing in Good News" for authoring thousands of stories about inspirational people and efforts that have a positive impact. Alicia is based in Southern California and is working on a children's book titled, appropriately, *Kid Gloves*.

Portrait taken by Kathy Cruts of me and Robert Ortiz in 2020 at Kid Gloves Boxing in Simi Valley, California.

ACKNOWLEDGMENTS

It was the year 2000 when I retired from boxing, leaving the limelight that came along with fighting as one of only a few hundred women in America competing in this male-dominated sport. Back then, I started writing about my first-hand experience in the ring, but my story never came to fruition, as my recount seemed trite, with no real depth behind what I considered my salvation. I needed to take a step back, put these pages aside, and deeply contemplate my battles in the ring—as well as the battles I overcame long before I earned my championship titles. This introspection took decades of taking a hard look at myself, and once I came through on the other side, I was ready to finally finish my first nonfiction novel about my boxing career. To say this task was difficult is an understatement, as I spent many days perplexed over the memories that poured out of my mind through my fingertips on the keyboard, solidifying my experiences into the written word. When my manuscript was finished, I didn't want to share it with anyone at first. Exposing my deepest pain made me too vulnerable. I didn't want anyone to know the person I used to be, the insecurities I keep hidden to this day, the inner battle I'm still fighting. But the people I love and trust felt otherwise. Without them, this book wouldn't be possible.

For years I've been told by loved ones that my story is worth telling, that vulnerability is something all humans share, and that the world's most influential and inspirational people are those who talk about their battles and adversities they overcame. Because of this, I was able to step outside of myself as a third-person observer, and write my story as though it happened to someone else. Once the words were written, I realized my story shouldn't be kept a secret, but shared. This work is the result of support and encouragement by those who never stopped believing in me, including my nephew, Trenton Doyle; my niece, Desiree Doyle Burgdorfer; my brother, Tony Doyle; my dad and stepmom, Frank and Patty Doyle; my aunt, Susie Joe; my former corner man, Robert Ortiz; my former coach, Stan Ward; my friends, Alexandra Lin Wiggins and Melinda Fulmer; and Diane Elizabeth Huntington Loring, the founder of Women Involved in Sports Evolution. I must also give credit to my opponents who gave their heart and soul to boxing and stepped in the ring with me, especially Layla McCarter, who taught me the value of sportsmanship.

Others who made this book possible include Rod Holcomb, a producer and director who first approached me in 2000 about turning my story into a movie; Ivor Davis, a best-selling author and boxing fan who encouraged me to finish my novel; Jose Ramirez of Pedernales Publishing, who helped me put together the intricate pieces of this memoir and bring it to fruition; Flo Selfman, owner of Words à la Mode who edited my work; and photographer Kathy Cruts, who came up with the visual concept that conveys vulnerability and strength in the portraits that appear in this book.

There are countless others who had a tremendous impact on my life, and without them, my story wouldn't exist. My mother, Patsy Kong, is one of the strongest women I know. The two brothers I grew up with made me feel safe during my childhood filled with fear and uncertainty. Ms. Pidgeon, the psychologist who mentored me when I was in grade school, has since passed away, but her spirit will remain forever in my heart.

For those of you whose names I didn't mention, know that you played a significant part in my journey, too, and I will never forget the valuable life lessons I learned from you.

Portrait taken by Kathy Cruts in 2020.

CPSIA information can be obtained
at www.ICGtesting.com
Printed in the USA
LVHW022133260523
748159LV00002B/416